MW01289473

BRUCE'S BELIEFS

Everything I know about business (and life), I learned playing with toys

BY

BRUCE D. LUND

CONTENTS

CONTENTS

INTRODUCTION

I have been a toy inventor for many years, and I have learned a few things along the way. Some I have discovered, some I have realized, and some I have come to believe  are true and important—for me, and perhaps for you. It is my hope that sharing some of what I have learned may enrich your life in some small way, and by extension, the lives of those around you.

I have begun a new chapter in my life, in which I do more and put off less. There is not as much time for procrastination now, don'tcha know? I make sure to do my yearly motorcycle tour, like a sacred ritual. My trip plans have become more ambitious over the years: I have biked around each of the five Great Lakes; I have begun a trip around the perimeter of the United States that will take three years to complete, riding two weeks or so each year, and I already have a broken leg to show for it. Then I'd like to ride the sixteen thousand miles from Alaska to Tierra del Fuego at the tip of South America. Then, perhaps, I'll ride across Australia.

I have taken up scuba diving and skydiving again after a long hiatus. It has been both scary and exhilarating. A couple of years ago, I took up roller-skating, and now spend hours each weekend honing my skills and techniques with the wind in my face, sweat soaked; racing around exuberantly dancing to the music on quad skates. I push myself until I am exhausted.

I do it all for me, and it is good.

This very book is another project I have long contemplated and have now finally realized. So why write a book? What have I learned that I yearn to share with you?

As I am in the business of creating truly great toys, I have discovered the impact that toys have on the lives of the children who play with them and on the contributions they will make to the world as they grow into adulthood. Frank Lloyd Wright and the Wright brothers both attest that their childhood toys inspired their life's work.

More broadly, my goal is to be excellent at what I do and to continuously improve in all aspects of my work and life. In my work, at least, I can see that progress. Life is messy, and improvement is difficult to gauge. I believe that excellence in all we do, both in our work and in our lives, is a worthy goal, and continuous improvement is the means to that end.

I believe that there is a law of intention and that what you think about or dream of, good or bad, desire or fear, will come to pass. I cannot quite explain this, but I see it at work, in my life, and in the lives of others around me. I believe we must guide our thoughts and dreams toward what we seek in life, and that we must always guard against fear and worry about anything negative that might happen instead. Allowing our minds to focus on potential negative events and outcomes will ensure that those fears and worries become real.

I believe that persistence and hard work overcome all. Overnight success takes twenty years. I try to be diligent and persistent in my efforts. As the water and the wind wear down the rock to create the Grand Canyon and a rocky mountain into gentle hills, so too our persistence over time overcomes challenges that we face and yields the successes we seek.

Persistence makes up for any shortfall I may have in intelligence, inherited wealth, creativity, or other God-given advantages others might have. Persistence alone is entirely in my control.

I believe that extraordinary effort yields extraordinary results. Working a forty-hour week is the legal minimum; therefore, you are likely to achieve the minimum results from that minimum level of effort. In that way, the universe is fair. What you get out is commensurate with what you put in, just as it should be.

I believe that teamwork is the secret to great results. It is colorless, tasteless, invisible to the eye, and yet teamwork is very real and of critical importance. The hallmarks of teamwork are generosity of spirit and respect for your collaborators.

I believe that life is a precious gift—the most precious. Life is ours to savor, to revel and delight in, to do good in the lives of others, and to make the world a better place.

There are other things, too, that I have learned, and I hope that the words that follow may benefit you in some small way.

Tips on how to read this book:

- Each of the beliefs in this book is a separate entity, loosely tied under a chapter heading's general theme. However, please keep in mind that there is some crossover and repetition between beliefs. I feel that some are just so important, they are worth repeating!

- I think you will find this book more enjoyable if you read it in snippets or one chapter at a time, as it is not meant to be read from cover to cover in one sitting. I see this book as a reference tool or personal guide to be absorbed and digested at different times in the day, the week, the month—whenever it is needed.

PREFACE

Why would anyone believe me?/aka why am I qualified to write this book?)

I got into the toy industry quite by accident. It was the summer of 1979 and I was unable to find an industrial design position anywhere in Chicago—and I tell you what, I tried everywhere! Someone suggested I contact Marvin Glass and Associates, the legendary Chicago-based toy invention studio. I had never heard of them or of toy design, but out of desperation, I called, got an appointment, and was invited back for a second interview.

I was broke at the time. I had $200 to my name, an old, beat-up Volvo, and my sewing machine from my years in the leather business. I had always been self-employed, so I didn't qualify for unemployment. I figured I would have to apply for welfare and food stamps, or starve. Pulling out all the stops, I cut my shaggy hair, took out my earring, and a guy named Harry Disko gave me my shot. Halleluiah! I will be eternally grateful to him and to Marvin Glass for the experience and opportunity they gave me.

I started immediately. I still remember seeing the extraordinary shop at Marvin Glass and Associates for the first time. It took my breath away. I had never seen anything like it before, and haven't since. Rows of beautifully painted, orange Bridgeport mills receded into the distance, and there were twin rows of bright yellow South Bend lathes and others by venerable machine tool brand names. These were the machines that built America and the world in the twentieth century.

The rows of machinery went on and on. Sanders, giant band saws, drill presses—bright, clean, and colorfully painted. Things I couldn't identify were sprinkled here and there; men were standing, working, and making chips and plastic dust at many of them. Others were hunched over their benches doing the handwork of toy creation. Many of the toys of our youths, now cultural icons, began in that shop—made on those machines, sprung from those benches like mushrooms in the night, created by displaced persons forced out of Europe after the war. Iconic toys and games like Mr. Machine, Lite-Brite, Rock 'Em Sock 'Em Robots, Operation, Mousetrap, Simon, and the list goes on….

There was equipment that I had never seen or heard of, and I had no idea what some did: vacuum metalizing, a full vinyl record recording studio, and hair rooting machines—un-freaking believable! Every machine was colorfully painted, looking far better than new. A new machine was drab green and gray, but here they were yellow, green, and orange. Wow! What a shop. Willy Wonka would have loved it. It was paradise.

I jumped right in and worked at Marvin Glass & Associates for five years. Then I decided that I knew more than the "partners" and forayed out on my own. Lund and Company took its first steps back in 1984 on my back porch in Roscoe Village, a cramped six-foot by ten-foot space under the EL tracks, with my father's old electric drill as my only power tool. To say that equipment was minimal would be an understatement. The resulting new products were equally unimpressive. I spent countless hours and days searching for inexpensive, used equipment. As a start-up, the company's money was tight. It would be tight again later, when the down years came upon us. But for a long time, the future was so bright, we had to wear shades.

By 1985, we were moving into our first real office and we needed everything. Inspired by Marvin Glass's extraordinary machine collection, I hunted for good deals on used machine tools, lathes, sanders, drill presses, mills, work tables, and desks. I crawled and squeezed my way through the dark and cavernous floors of Kaji's warehouses (a well-known local salvager), which were loaded to overflowing with the industrial machinery and office equipment he bought at auction. Somewhere in those warehouses, everything was to be had, haggled over, moved, and installed.

I later realized that all the time I spent searching was a trade-off, and maybe not such a good one, for the lower prices I got on the equipment. Time is money, but unlike money, it is irreplaceable. It is easy to squander it in the interest of saving a few dollars.

We soon moved into proper office space on Sunnyside and Ravenswood on one of Chicago's remaining brick surface roads, nestled between the EL tracks and the Illinois Central tracks. It was a quiet, industrial section in the heart of the city. We were growing now, having hired a model maker, artist, and two designers. Our game *Fireball Island* was a hit. Many more followed it, including the *Luminator Light-Up Foam Football* and sports line, an industry first; *Baby Alive Sip 'n Slurp*, and *Vac-Man*, the first toy industry application of "vacuumatic" technology.

By 1992, we bought and renovated our own building across the street from the boatyard and the Chicago River. The move provided thirty-five hundred square feet of office, conference, and show rooms. We now had a large, open, sunlight-filled studio workspace filled with machinery and equipment for building all manner of prototypes, toys for reference, drawers of motors, boxes of mechanisms, gears, magnets, and more—much, much more!

By 2007, we had once again outgrown our space. We hired architects and designed an award-winning building and workspace that would inspire and motivate our team to do the very best and most innovative work possible. Our current office is meant to be a "wow," a breathtaking experience for everyone who visits and everyone who works with us. As I approach the midpoint of my career, the new workspace inspires me to do the best work of my professional life.

What's the future for our team at Lund and Company Invention, L.L.C.? Can't say for sure, but I like what we're doing and the new directions we are exploring. That's a big part of what makes what we do so much fun and so exciting. Today, we are better than ever. I have rededicated myself to our work and to doing the best work of my life in the decades to come. I believe strongly that this commitment and renewal will be contagious!

So, here we go: I will give it my best shot to give you something of value in the pages to follow, to share some of the beliefs that I have learned and embraced. Thirty-plus years in the toy business have taught me a lot of life lessons applicable to the pursuit of business and personal success. And I hope that by the time you arrive at the last page of this book, you, too, will have learned a thing or two—and that you'll agree that my over three decades in the toy business has qualified me to write it (and that my career has certainly been a wild ride)!

CHAPTER I

BELIEF #1:

Toys Change The World

Belief #2:

We Are Influenced By The Playthings Of Our Youth

I'll bet you $100 that you didn't know that **toys change the world**. Toys are fundamentally different from every other type of product. Toys are the wellspring, the fountainhead, the source, and headwaters of inspiration. Childhood toys influence adulthood decisions, leading to innovation and the continuing evolution of modern civilization. Toys spawn advancements in science and technologies of every sort. Please allow me to explain.

The legendary architect Frank Lloyd Wright credits his kindergarten wooden block set as his inspiration to become an architect, and it is clear they influenced his design aesthetic, as well.

The Wright brothers attribute their calling to pursue powered flight to a wooden toy airplane, a birthday gift from their father.

Airplanes enable us to travel the world over. But it is the gift of a toy airplane that inspired two young men (bicycle mechanics, no less) to be fascinated by flight—and as adults, to pioneer modern air travel! Architects design all manner of buildings, but architecture was changed forever by a set of blocks that inspired a boy to become a revolutionary master in his field.

Any consumer product performs a function, but a toy has the power to inspire innovators, artists, designers, scientists, and engineers to do work in their lives that could one day change the world. Perhaps you recall childhood playthings that have influenced your choices as an adult. Possibly, they have influenced your choice of work and the impact you will have on the world in your lifetime.

It is possible to see the influences toys have played in the life work of artists, world leaders, scientists, innovators, and visionaries, across the world and across centuries. We are influenced by our playthings of youth, and that influence stretches through our lives, our work, and ultimately changes the world.

Belief #3:

What We Do In Play, We Become As Adults

We all start life as discoverers. Until we are old enough to be taught, we each explore and discover the world for ourselves. We discover that when we cry, Mom and Dad will take care of us. We discover that if we drop something, it will fall. We learn how the dog will respond if we pull on its ear. We learn how our sister will respond if we pull on her hair. We discover the rules of human behavior and the laws of nature.

Early childhood is one long, continual process of discovery, or self-learning. As we grow up, it seems, we discover fewer and fewer things for ourselves. Years of formal education teach us to learn from other sources rather than from our own observations and intrinsic processes of discovery. Or perhaps as we age, we form inflexible opinions and make the world fit our preconceptions rather than continually seek to refine our knowledge and under-standing of people, life, and the world.

Good toys are an important part of this early discovery process. Through play, children experiment with and discover for them-selves the workings of the physical world as well as how to interact with others, both adults and children. Through game play in par-ticular, we discover the unwritten rules of social behavior: what works well and what does not.

All human knowledge starts with discovery. Through discovery the world is changed in small and profound ways. Toys encourage and enable the discovery process; ergo, toys change the world!

I was fascinated with model rockets when I was in junior high and, I hate to admit, continued to be through high school. I loved the processes of designing, building, and then launching them in the cold, gray stillness of a winter's dawn. I spent many hours build-ing and spray-painting rockets in my father's basement workshop and many an early morning in farmers' fields launching them. I have been a morning person ever since.

One of my great contributions to society may have been the mounting of an M-80 in the nose of a rocket so that the parachute ejection charge would light the fuse. This was pure high school geek genius! The sound sleep of many people was disrupted by the overhead detonation and thunderclap of these childhood favorites. I could have lost an eye or a hand or ended up incarcerated on more than one occasion, but fortune favors the foolish at times. I have loved things that go BOOM! ever since.

There's no doubt in my mind: childhood playthings can and do become instrumental in one's adult work. Playing with rockets as a child inspired me to do the work I do today. Our *Hydrogen-Powered Rocket System* is one small example. It was the first new rocket system in fifty years, according to Estes, the original black powder rocket company—and they would certainly know! While it did not garner much media attention, it was an entirely new technology for hobby rockets and for the toy industry overall. It was also the first consumer product to produce and use hydrogen. First, it creates Hydrogen and Oxygen from water, using D-cell batteries. When a spark ignites the mixture of resulting gases, H_2 and O_2 then recombine very suddenly into water, instantaneously releasing the energy that was put into separating the gases initially. This explosion will launch a toy rocket or power an internal combustion engine. You just have to love things that go boom!

The toy rocket led us to explore and develop many other Hydrogen-powered products, including a *Radio-Controlled Vehicle System,* which won an award in a NASA-sponsored technology competition. From that project, we designed a *Hydrogen-Powered Lawn Mower* for the Chicago Parks District, teaming up with the Illinois Institute of Technology and John Deere. The plan was to use the *Hydrogen-Powered Lawn Mower* in the city parks and show the world that Chicago was a leader in the green energy movement.

So, do I maintain that toys are profoundly important to the world? YES, I DO! Not just to children, but to the advancement of society. I believe that toys are the most important category of product, period. Other products may serve useful functions, but only toys inspire us to change the world as adults.

This is the message we who have the privilege of working in the toy industry might do well to internalize: the creation of new toys and games is important work, and what we do matters. The toy industry has the opportunity and responsibility to create great products that will influence and inspire the next generation and the future of our culture.

Belief #4:
Baby Dolls Are The Reason For Life On This Planet

Through play and toys we discover our interests and abilities, as well as develop our innate selves. I believe the nurturing instinct of females is developed and encouraged through nurturing play patterns, like playing with baby dolls. Nurturing play patterns balance the aggressive, combat play patterns favored by boys that encourage their inherently more aggressive, violent natures.

While one might wish it were not so, the world around us is evidence aplenty of the elemental difference between the male and female natures, in all manner of animal species. Males and females are different, and among mammals it is the female that nurtures the young, even protecting them from the male in many cases.

Of course, there are exceptions, as there are to every rule, but exceptions do not obviate the rule. They are only exceptions. Personal preference plays no part in making it so, or not so. Gravity is unaffected by our opinion of it. Likewise, whether one likes the idea of elementally different natures of males and females, it makes no difference to the existence of those differences.

This nurturing, feminine force in today's world, encouraged and developed through nurturing play patterns such as with baby dolls, has kept us from pushing the button and assuring our mutual destruction. The cultures that most oppress women and suppress that nurturing influence offer the greatest threat to our modern civilization. In western cultures in particular, this influence of women in their society is greater, and that nurturing aspect of the female psyche acts as a counterbalance.

Hence, it may be that dolls, and baby dolls in particular, are the reason that life continues on earth today. We have designed many successful dolls, including *Baby Alive Sip 'n Slurp, Baby Go Boom* (and by the way, that is a reference to the baby doll falling on her bum, not an explosion as some incorrectly perceived), *Little Mommy Baby Knows,* and more. Each is entertaining and fun to play with; and each allows the exploration, development, expression, and enhancement of girls' nurturing spirits, providing balance in modern western civilization.

Belief #5:
Toys Exercise The Mind And Body

In Norman Brosterman's book, *Inventing Kindergarten,* [Brosterman 1997] you will find compelling examples of the profound influence of the set of educational "gifts" from the kindergarten program (we would call them toys or activity toys) on the work of many who were directly or indirectly inspired by them. This includes, notably, many of the twentieth century's greatest artists, designers, architects, and visionaries.

According to Brosterman, one of the gifts of the original European kindergarten system may well have inspired the Cubism style in painting. The work of Mondrian and other artists of the era appear to have been influenced by other toys and activities in that system. A cultural archeologist like Brosterman, seeking the origins and inspirations of seminal works in different fields of endeavor, concludes similarly about one field after another.

Even many contemporaries who did not go through the system were inevitably exposed to it. For those who are unsure about the importance of toys in modern society, this section of Brosterman's book is a must-read.

Nobel-prize-winning scientist Sir Harry Kroto once remarked in a BBC radio interview (as reported in *Popular Science* [Benson 2010]) that one of the disasters of modern life is that the Erector Set has been displaced by Legos. In his opinion, the relatively simple block, replacing the far more complex nuts, bolts, girders, and beams of the Erector/Meccano system has resulted in a great loss to society. Now, we all agree that Legos are great. But his point is that children's imaginations are not as challenged by Legos' block-stacking play as they would be by the complex play and resulting possibilities that the Erector set offers. More generally, this scientist's point supports mine: toys matter to the world and to all of us. That is just what the toy industry needs to be saying— including its inventors, designers, marketers, advertising, public relations (PR) executives, and sales reps. What the toy industry does is important!

Creating and bringing toys to market is like delivering nutritious food to the brains of children everywhere to help them grow and develop to their greatest potentials. This matters, because the brains we are feeding will one day feed the world.

In a great article from the *New York Times* on September 2, 2009, [Brown 2009] Stuart Brown comments on the decline of active play in children's lives and the beneficial, even essential influence of play on human development. Without play, a child cannot grow up to be a normal, healthy adult. And of course, toys are an agent of play and the normal, healthy development of the human spirit and psyche.

Brown cites a University of Michigan study [Juster 2004] that found that children at that time were spending half as much time playing outside as they had twenty years earlier. Instead, they spent an average of more than six hours each day with electronic media, in front of some kind of electronic screen. I am concerned about this, as I'm sure many are. Brown makes the case that there is a connection between the decrease in outdoor play time and the great increase in childhood obesity, ADHD, childhood depression, and other social maladies.

Can it be that toys and play are just what the doctor ordered for a healthy, well-adjusted child? The toy industry should be shouting from the rooftops the critical importance and extraordinary benefits children reap from simply playing with toys.

As Brown suggests in the *New York Times* article, we need a "change in public consciousness about play— to show that it is not trivial or elective." This change in public perception and awareness on the critical importance of play can and should start with the toy industry, toy companies—perhaps first with Toys "R" Us and other toy retailers.

Play is extremely, critically, essentially important to the health of a child and the health of the adult each child will become.

Belief #6:
A Game Is A Machine For Human Interaction

Belief #7:
Games Teach Skills Not Taught Elsewhere

My definition of a game is "a machine for human interaction." Whether by card or die, ball or board, the activity of playing a game engenders, encourages, and creates the interpersonal communication we call "fun." It is hard to define precisely what fun is, but we know it when we see it or experience it ourselves. Fun is the magic that happens in the air between people and above the actual game equipment.

A board game is a machine for human interaction in that it enables an enjoyable interplay between people, somehow, someway. It is magical. What makes a game great is a mystery to me. Unlike a toy, the magic is in the interactions of the players and does not reside in the device itself.

Our game *Fireball Island* is considered a cult classic and one of the best board games of the 1980s. Another Lund game, *Dragon Strike*, was named Game of the Year in Austria, a country where games are revered and treasured, much as they are in Germany. And the more recent *Doggie Doo Game* was named 2011 Game of the Year in France and London! *Fireball Island* was inspired by a 3-D, distortion-printed, vacuum-formed map (quite a mouthful—it won't be on the test!), and *Dragon Strike* was inspired by the cheap, wiggly, plastic, segmented carnival snake toy that you have all seen and played with when you were a kid.

Fireball Island was one of our first products we did way back when we first started out. (I use the royal "we," as it was pretty much just me working on it at the time.) It was a hit and still has followers still to this day. I sculpted the original prototype in clay; slush molded it, and struggled with it for weeks, maybe months. It was originally called *Fireball Mountain,* but it was indeed an island. The final, hand-built prototype was very close to what Milton Bradley licensed from us, with a few differences. Instead of caves, a helicopter flew a player from landing site to landing site on the island. At first, it was dreadfully boring to play, until my best friend Randy (may God rest his soul) made some suggestions. The changes radically improved game play, and suddenly it became an intensely fun experience. Play *Fireball Island* if you ever get the chance. You'll love it! And don't just take it from me; here are some quotes from actual fans:

"I truly love that game. It has brought tons of joy to my life. I love sharing it with people who have never played. We even played it this year during the family Christmas get-together and it was a huge hit. Thank you so much for creating Fireball Island!"

"OMG you are the inventor of FIREBALL ISLAND? I LOVED that game when I was a kid!"

"Wait, you made Fireball Island? WOW! Quite frankly, one of the best board games ever created."

"I had that game, and I did love it. It vanished some years ago from my collection. Thanks for the fun memories!"

"Fireball Island is one of the most fun games ever!"

Game playing is a very important medium through which kids, and thereby adults, learn about important life concepts. These include fairness, competition, playing by the rules, the benefits of losing (and winning) gracefully, the consequences of cheating or other ill-advised behaviors, the pain of losing, and the joy of winning. Games teach us, as children, many important lessons not learned elsewhere or otherwise.

Belief #8:
Laughter Heals, Restores, And Renews

Great toys need to elicit some form of visceral, instinctive response from the user. Great toys will:

- Astound and amaze (the "Oh, Wow!" factor)

- Make you laugh hysterically (a few chuckles won't cut it)

- Grab your heartstrings, and make girls go "Oh-ooh," that sing-songy, two-syllable sound they make. (I love it when they do that!) In other words, be achingly cute and adorable!

Our *TMX Elmo* achieved the first two. It astounded and amazed, as well as made young and old laugh 'til they cried! A friend told me the story of an autistic child who had not spoken in three years, but who laughed when he played with *TMX Elmo*. Another friend related a story of a woman he knew who was grieving from the recent loss of her husband. He watched as she took out her granddaughter's *TMX Elmo* and it instantly lifted her mood. She explained that she often did that when she was feeling particularly sad and that it always made her feel better. That is the power of laughter.

Through *TMX Elmo*, we have been reawakened to the power of laughter. We have learned that laughter is one of the most powerful forces in nature; that it comforts, heals, and just plain makes us all feel better. It is a powerful force in a world that is sometimes lacking in mirth, humor, and the good-old-fashioned guffaw.

Toys make people laugh, probably more than any other type of product. Laughter does a body good. Make sure you laugh with someone today!

Belief #9:
Cherish Your Childhood Toys

Like you, no doubt, I have many fond memories of my favorite childhood toys and games. How many can you recall?

I loved playing the Diners Club game and the Hardy Boys game, hardly classics either one, but we played them again and again, and again, and again, and again, and…you get the picture.

The Marx Fort Apache play set was another favorite that provided hours on end of play: setting up the stockade, and then arranging and rearranging the characters. I longed to have some of the other Marx play sets. As a family, we played Scrabble, and I still have that very same game, with most of its wooden letter tiles.

Other favorites were die-cast Dinky toys (these were like Matchbox cars on steroids), mostly army vehicles, and a plethora of smaller die-cast Matchbox cars and trucks that my mother would bring back from Canada after visiting her mother and sisters. I spent hundreds of hours playing with them, perhaps more. Now those were indeed great toys!

I would spend entire summers playing in the dirt with big steel trucks, bull dozers, graders, excavators, and others that my father would get me. With the building of the Robert Moses power plant just a few miles away, as well as the similarly named parkways, major construction went on in my neighborhood for most of my childhood. Emulating that construction in my own play, with trucks big and small, was a favorite pastime—when we weren't playing baseball, football, or basketball, that is.

Model kits were another favorite, but more to build and destroy than to display. I encouraged my friends to bring out their model ships and we would send World War II battleships down rain-swollen ditches. We peppered them with BB gun fire, attempting to sink them, or dropped firecrackers on the decks to simulate war scenes. There's nothing better than things that blow up!

I was not a very good model kit builder. My model cars always seemed to have fingerprints melted into the windshields that had been softened by too much styrene glue. The paint jobs were dreadful, as I recall. But the models were great to douse in lighter fluid and to watch roll down a hill, flames shooting in the air, until the tires melted and the entire vehicle became a burning puddle of liquid plastic! Oh, for those simple pleasures of childhood.

In my teen years, M-80s became the go-to "toy" of choice. Oh, the things you can do with an M-80! These illegal fireworks were hard to acquire, so we were delighted to discover that farmer's co-ops sold them as "agricultural pest control bombs." Making up the unlikely story that we needed them for "low-level atmospheric research for science projects," we were able to obtain a gross of them. One hundred forty-four M-80s: imagine it! It was really more than we could have dared to hope for.

Imagine all the scenarios: Drop them into a cinder block and watch it crack. Tie some to a rock and throw it into a lake; watch for a flash below the surface, the shock wave, and then smoky bubbles coming to the surface along with a fish or two. Stand in the bow of a speeding aluminum outboard motorboat, trying to light and throw them (unsuccessfully) at seagulls…never realizing that they could end up back in the boat by mistake.

At night, one might launch them by slingshot high into the air and over the woods, beyond which a camp full of young Girl Guides slumbered—until their sleep was shattered by the sudden "Ba-boom!" of an M-80 way overhead. Crazy stuff "one" might do with an M-80.

But a close call might end all that nonsense. For example: if, perchance, the rubber band on the slingshot were to break while one had it drawn fully back next to one's ear while pinching tightly a ready-to-launch M-80 with a rapidly burning fuse. One really could lose an eye, one's hearing, or even a hand playing with these things. Amazingly, we survived unscathed, though we had many a close call. If my mother had ever found out what we were doing, we would have been in BIG trouble. But better for her that she never knew.

Even better, we discovered that an M-80, placed fuse-down in the nose of a model rocket, would be ignited by the rocket engine's parachute ejection charge. It would coast upward and then down, and explode far overhead. 'Tis a beautiful thing indeed, 'tis a fireball way up high in the sky. But if the time delay on the rocket engine was long enough, the "ba-boom" would occur much closer to the ground.

Once, quite by accident, the wind caught one of these M-80 warhead-equipped rockets out over the lake at my good friend's cottage. It drifted downwind over the next property, where a hundred innocent Girl Guides were in the water, swimming under their counselors' watchful eyes. (I know what you're thinking, and you're right. Sheer stupidity on our part, I know, but the adolescent brain was still developing. That's all I can offer by way of explanation and apology, Mrs. Officer. We were dumb and dumber.)

Crap! With a capital "K"! Oh no!

This particular rocket engine had a long time delay, and we watched with dread as the warhead-equipped rocket arced over at the apogee of its trajectory and began to head straight down, toward the unsuspecting girls frolicking in the lake!

Fearing the worst, we gathered up our incriminating rocket stuff and ran as fast as our little legs could carry us. Fifty feet overhead, the M-80 finally detonated. A hundred simultaneous screams, yelling, ranting girls stampeding out of the water—Oy vey! Thankfully, none were hurt, but many felt terrorized.

And then one day, the M-80s disappeared. And my mother didn't know a thing about it, ever. So maybe, somehow, she did find out. Hmmmmm…I'd always thought they would turn up. They never did.

CHAPTER II

BELIEF #10:

Toys Matter

Belief #11:
Free Play Is Essential To A Child

The *American Journal of Play* [Gray Spring 2011] devoted an entire issue to scholarly articles addressing the subject of free play—as opposed to structured play, organized sports, and the like. One article was about the consequences of our fearful attitudes toward the world and its dangers to children—essentially that they reduced free play, like the play I engaged in when I was a kid in the streets, backyards, fields, forests, and vacant lots, for endless days on end. Free play has many benefits.

In another article in the series, the anthropologist Peter Gray examines rule making and rule breaking and the benefits of children playing outside the realm of adult oversight. He considers the reduction in Free Play to be the cause of the steep rise in the psychopathology of children and adolescents.

Gray also examines play habits across various species of mammals and the similarities they bear to human children's play. For example, childcare and nurturing play can be seen in primate as well as human female offspring, while more rough-and-tumble play is common in the male young across species. This rough-and-tumble play is useful for learning to regulate one's emotions.

Play has been shown to stimulate genes for nerve growth in the executive portion of the brain. After a thirty-minute play session, perhaps as many as four hundred genes exhibit activation and are "significantly modified." The non-directed, non-goal-oriented activity we call play enhances the brain development needed for later goal-directed activities. In other words, play develops our ability to regulate ourselves and to pursue goals with directed, focused activity as adults.

Play promotes children's mental health in the following ways:
- Play helps kids develop interests and competencies.

- Play helps children learn to follow rules, make decisions, regulate their own behavior, and solve problems.

- Play helps a child learn how to make friends and to treat others as equals.

- Through play, a child experiences joy.

What does it all mean?

An interesting insight from Mr. Gray, and I paraphrase slightly, is that social play is nature's way of teaching young humans that they are not special. Even those who are more skilled than others at games or activities must consider the others' wants and needs as equal to their own, or face being excluded from the play altogether.

Play is essential. Play is crucial, critical, of paramount importance to the raising of a child. Toys are important tools of play. Toys enable play; toys are the implements around which play is organized. Toys help children experience joy and help them learn how to make and keep friends. Toys are tools through which children learn how to make decisions, regulate their own behavior, and follow rules.

Toys help develop the imagination. They are essential components of a child's happiness and good mental health. By enabling play, toys have been essential in all of our own healthy upbringings and have enabled us to function successfully in the world today as adults.

In other words, toys matter.

BELIEF #12:
Play Engenders Life Skills

When did you last have the privilege of watching a child at play?

I had the opportunity recently to watch a two-year-old boy playing with his toy cars. "MINE!" he yells emphatically as he holds an armful of them to his chest. It appears that he has just acquired the concept of ownership, and with his armful of toy cars, he is rich.

I have watched this little boy, Bartholomew Buckwaltersonburgsenski (not his real name), play hour upon hour and day after day with a cute little pull-back, wind-up car not much bigger than his fist. I never realized those were such great toys: I am astonished at how much play value a simple toy can have. Bart pulls the car back and watches it roll slowly forward on the floor, then on the arm of a chair or on the table where another person turns it around and sends it back, on the counter top to watch it roll off and fall to the ground, on the (very patient) dog, on the couch, back on the table, on the stereo, and on and on it goes.

I have watched this child play day after day with several die-cast vehicles of different scales. He lines them up in a row, side by side. He rolls them along, and he carries an armload of them around the house, clutched close like something precious—and to him, they are.

I have watched him play for hours upon hours with a large plastic dump truck of some sort—ramming it hundreds of times into the baseboards and anything else that won't get out of its way. When he plays with that toy, the dog is constantly on the move to stay out of the way. The truck goes rocketing across the floor on its own, or it is pushed along at a recklessly high rate of speed, as if life itself depended on it.

Toys are precious in the life of a child. As adults, we often can't appreciate how precious these treasured toys are to a child. Or maybe we can, if we just think back…

BELIEF #13:

Toys Are Sacred Relics Of Childhood

At their best, toys can be the most cherished and loved possessions of a child's life. Next to my motorcycles, those few favorite, treasured toys I had as a child are still my favorites. Toys have something almost sacred about them. They are like the royal crown jewels of England, but even more precious and loads more fun.

What about you? Were toys special in your life? Were they cherished and treasured? Are they still?

Toys are not like other consumer goods. The products we create in the toy business are meaningfully different. They become the sacred relics of our childhoods, and indeed, of our lives.

I ran across a photo of a long, long-ago Christmas, and in it is one of my favorite toys from childhood: a play set my father made for my Matchbox vehicles. It was inspired by the decades-long construction project of the Robert Moses Power Authority near where I grew up in Lewiston, NY.

The play set had a wood frame and was sculpted with chicken wire covered with a compound of sawdust and wood glue painted gray to look like solid rock, and it had black roads. The yule fire burns in the background of the photo, with the handmade stockings all hung with care above it. I am awaiting St. Nicholas, who soon would be there. In fact, upon a closer look, the stockings appear to have things in them—oranges and apples, no doubt—I surmise that this photo was actually taken later that Christmas day, and that this play set was the highlight of that long-ago Christmas morn. I even remember the coconut that sat on the hearth, though I have no idea why it was there or where it had come from. I wish I could climb into that picture and look around at the rest of my childhood home all decorated for Christmas on this magical day so long ago, now lost in time.

The play set had three levels for my construction vehicles, connected by steep roads cut into the rock; a bridge made of wood, with wire rails; and a metal-roofed garage. Hours, months, even years of play did I have with that play set, so perfect was it—the product of a father's love for a son. It was a toy that no doubt inspired me to do what I have done now for some thirty years and counting, in the endeavor to create toys as wonderful as the one that my father made for me so very long ago.

BELIEF #14:

If Games Go Digital, We Lose

Games go digital? What happened? Major game companies bemoan the downward pressure on retail prices, and lament the fact that games are going digital. It is parents who buy games for the family, and Moms and Dads are on Facebook playing Farmville, instead of combing the toy aisles for good, old-fashioned family game entertainment.

Hmmmm. I don't like the sound of that. So are games to go totally digital? Spending $1 for an addictive game app I can play anywhere seems like a great value compared to $24.95 for a real-world board or plastic action game. While you do pay $50 per month to maintain the device for which you paid hundreds of dollars to own, the added value of the game is great and the additive cost is minimal.

But if something is gained, then what is lost? Facebook and smartphone app games are no substitute for face-to-face, hand-to-hand, head-to-head game play, whether on the field, the floor, or the table.

The value of face-to-face game play is no longer widely appreciated. The values are many, in fact, including not just the social aspects of cooperation, competition, following rules, and so on, but also the physical, fine and gross motor skills, logic, and more. Another great point of these types of games is their flexibility and the opportunity they offer for players to be creative by modifying the play of the game. But yes, we need new and better ways to market our real-world games that make them as easy to acquire as new smart phone apps.

One thing is for certain: change is afoot, and more than one factor is surely at work. The game makers, designers, and inventors need to wake up and smell the cardboard (or the electrons, perhaps. Oh, I love the smell of electrons in the morning)! We all need to embrace change, or die. Say, where did I hear that before?

At the very least, we all need to hear the wake-up-call and take a hard look at what we are doing and how it is working, and use it as the incentive to get better at what we do. Now is the opportunity to ride the dangerous wind, to create better, more engaging games, more fun products, more diverse, better-promoted, better-marketed, better products, distributed and retailed in new and better ways.

Hook 'em horns. Circle the wagons. Darn the torpedoes. Full speed ahead. Grab the bull by the horns, and so on and et cetera. Know what I mean?

CHAPTER III

BELIEF #15:

Imagination Changes Everything

Belief #16:
Imagine What You Seek, And You Will Find It

What we imagine and focus on will come to pass, good or bad. If we imagine success, we will experience success. If we imagine failure, we will experience failure. If we imagine happiness, we will experience happiness. Keep your mind's eye trained on where you want to go, on the goals you want to achieve, and the mental state in which you want to exist.

Imagination is a powerful force, not just in creating insanely great new products, but more importantly, in shaping our future. When you are riding a motorcycle, the bike will go where you are looking, whether you really want to go there or not. If you don't keep your eyes on the road, your bike will wander off as well. This same principle applies in businesses and in life. Our lives will follow where we look and will turn out the way we visualize them.

Long ago, I was in the leatherwork business, living in a little shotgun house in Durham, North Carolina. I stumbled upon Victor Papanek's book, *Design for the Real World,* [Papanek 2005] and was inspired to study product design as an avenue to becoming an inventor. I wanted to invent things, though I didn't know what, and I wanted my products to be sold around the world.

Longwinded story made short, I went to the Institute of Design in Chicago, received my MS in industrial design, and by a miracle was hired by a toy invention company after I had almost given up my search for a job as a designer. I have made my living as an inventor for more than thirty years, and as I had long ago imagined, the products that my team and I create are sold around the world. I did not set out to create products that would be sold worldwide, but I imagined it, desired it, and it came true. In many ways, my life has become what I long ago imagined, without working consciously toward those imagined outcomes. I am proof that what we imagine is what will be.

The bike goes where the eyes look. Keep your eyes (and your imagination) on the road. Imagine what you seek, and you may find it. Imagine what you fear, and you may find that too.

Simple choice. Look, and think, where you want to go.

Belief #17:
Like A Muscle, Exercise Imagination To Make It Stronger

Once upon a time, there was a final examination in Physics class, and the teacher observed that his best student seemed to be stuck. The student was scratching his head, playing with his pencil, and looking around, so the teacher walked over to inquire what had him so perplexed.

The student was stuck on a problem that asked him to determine the height of a tall building using a barometer. The teacher inquired what his best student was thinking, since the obvious and only solution was to use the device to measure the difference in barometric pressure at the top and bottom of the building, and then calculate from there.

Or maybe not.

"Well," the young scholar replied, "There are so many possible answers that I don't know which one to choose. For example, I could take the barometer to the top of the building and drop it off, timing how long it takes to hit the ground, and thereby calculate the height of the building. Or, I could tie a string to the barometer and let it down to the sidewalk from the top of the building, bring it back up, and measure the length of the string to determine the building's height. Or, I could find the building supervisor, and tell him, I will give you this really nice barometer if you will tell me the height of this building."

Now that is imaginative thinking! By looking at a problem upside down or sideways, we can come up with new solutions that would not occur to us otherwise.

Believing in Santa Claus is good for you, because it is an example of imaginative and magical thinking. It is exercise for the imagination. Like a muscle, if you exercise the imagination, you make it stronger. I came across a *Wall Street Journal* (Wang 2009) article about the power of magical thinking and its benefits for children and adults.

Exercising the imagination strengthens, develops, builds, and otherwise enhances imaginative power, just as exercising strengthens and builds muscles. Research has shown that children who are prone to believing in the imaginary reap other positive benefits that follow them into adulthood. Toys are tools for developing the power of imagination.

At Lund and Company Invention, we are passionate about what we do. We wallow like pigs in the mud in the processes of imagination and creation, experimentation and tinkering, discovery, challenge, and problem solving.

Our office is more like a laboratory than a design studio. We make things move, bring things to life in new ways, create and develop new technologies, and imbue products with personality, scripting, and play patterns. Wondrous things seem to spring up from our workbenches like mushrooms overnight.

What we do is more like a special-effects house than a design studio. We make mechanical magic controlled by electronic magic, and the end result amazes, entertains, and in some cases, astonishes. We work hard at exercising those imaginative muscles every single day. And we hope and pray that playing with our toys helps develop the imaginations of millions upon millions of kids—and adults as well.

Belief #18:
Everything Starts With An Idea

I suspect that important ideas, ideas that have real impact, such as the Panama Canal, the Great Pyramids, the Interstate Highway System, and the Human Genome Project have all been roundly criticized and even denounced or ridiculed.

I cannot count the number of times I have been told something will not work, cannot be done, or is a waste of time, only to find that our team was able to accomplish it. Indeed, I have been guilty of that myself on countless occasions, critiquing the ideas of others or believing something was impossible that I later found possible by dint of hard work and the suspension of disbelief.

Everything starts with an idea: just a thought; delicate and ephemeral, like a bubble. Ideas, like tiny seeds, need fertile earth and nurturing to survive and grow. Good ideas, like seeds, can be remarkably tough and durable and sit waiting until conditions are favorable for growth. In fact, the test of a good idea may just be this waiting period.

We tend to get infatuated with our ideas. I liken it to seeing a pretty girl and falling "in love" instantly, willing to sacrifice a knuckle, a finger, a limb just to…hmmm…with her. But then another comes along, and one instantly forgets the first and falls into infatuation with a new one, and on and on. None of these infatuations should lead to marriage without a significant passage of time and a study of the individual to see if they are worth investing one's life in. We should approach ideas likewise.

We tend to fall in love with our own ideas just the same, and waiting can be a useful way to see how strong the infatuation with any one idea really is. We call it "marinating." Let ideas sit awhile and marinate, and come back to them later when the infatuation has passed to see how much you truly love them. If they pass that test, they deserve more time and attention.

Everything starts with just an idea, a thought; but like peanut butter and jelly (or chocolate and peanut butter), concept and execution complement each other and are equally important. I am often taken aback by the beauty of the execution of some new concept.

A new idea may be terrific, but the art and craft of what we do, the physical translation of an idea into reality, is like the work of an artist or a fine craftsperson. Coming from a craft tradition, I am keenly aware and appreciative of the skill and aesthetic sensitivity involved in making a beautiful thing.

On one side are the invention, ideas, and concepts taking shape in the imagination. On the other are the science of exploring, testing, tinkering, and discovery, followed by the art and craft of creation: making the idea real and instantly appealing to those to whom we present it.

Sometimes the art is in a small physical detail, like a tiny pair of handmade, simulated wire-rim glasses. Other times it might be in the beautiful shipping carton made just for the product and its various and sundry pieces. Often, the art lies in the elegance and richness of the programming and play patterns with which we have imbued the product.

But in the end, everything starts with just an idea.

Belief #19:
Ideas Are The Most Powerful Force In The World

Ideas are the most powerful force in the world. They are the wellspring of all we know and do, touch and feel—of our entire world.

History can be boring until you stand where it played out and can see for yourself the product of imagination, innovation, engineering, vision, persistence, and hard work. I once stumbled across the museum of a long-defunct canal that transformed the region of the Catskills in the early 1800s. Before the advent of railroads, only waterways, natural and manmade, could economically carry ores and other bulk products long distances.

Sources of energy have always excited the imagination and plans of entrepreneurs. When the original black gold, anthracite coal, was discovered in the western section of the Catskill Mountains in the 1800s, coal had to be transported from its source over the hills to a port where it was carried by ship to far-off destinations.

It required imagination, innovation, engineering, vision, persistence, and hard work aplenty to create a canal 108 miles long, going up the western face of the mountain and back down the other side, even crossing over several rivers. A total of 108 locks raised and lowered the water level eight to twelve feet at each lock, allowing the mules and their walk-beside mule-tenders (generally young children from orphanages) to pull the hundred-ton ore barges the 108 miles up and over and back down the eleven hundred feet of elevation changes. This canal was truly a miracle of imagination and innovation, and was in use for over seventy years.

Before the advent of the steam locomotive, people used tracked cars and "gravity railroads" to winch ore car trains up hills and brake-control them back down, a system that resulted in many spectacular crashes.

To cross rivers and chasms, people built aqueducts—bridges for water—over which the mules, muleskinners, and the barges they pulled could move at one to three miles per hour. These aqueducts were designed by Roebling, the legendary engineer who later designed the Brooklyn Bridge.

Standing on the sites of the visionary, imaginative, innovative, and astonishingly inventive accomplishments of those who created these systems, one is struck with wonder. There is such a rich history of inventive thinking in this country alone.

Henry F. Phillips, a more contemporary innovator, invented and licensed the Phillips-head screw after being rejected by almost all the screw makers of the time who said it couldn't be made. It was a better solution for many reasons, and someone finally figured out how to make it a reality.

Mr. Phillips' story is much like that of Colonel Sanders and his secret fried chicken recipe he spent years of his life trying to sell. He traveled across the country and lived in his car, relentlessly pitching until he finally sold it. He did one thing, and he did it right.

Similarly, a man and a woman from Idaho had an idea and little more than two nickels to rub together. It was an idea so outlandish, so big, that anyone with a lick of sense would discount it out of hand—my (short-sighted and limited-in-imagination) self included. This couple imagined the highways of America with solar panels incorporated into them to generate electricity and support the somewhat fragile national electric grid.

They envisioned roadways with LED lights embedded in them to become endless LED displays, providing signage warning of accidents up ahead, changing lane markers, displaying speed limits, or moving traffic over and around roadside hazards. With the University of Michigan as a partner to create a translucent roadway surface, and with the Department of Transportation funding them, the couple is now on the way to demonstrating the large-scale feasibility of this idea for highways of the future.

I still can't believe it. An idea from way out in Idaho, a li'l ol' thought that occurs to a man and a woman, not a research lab or an invention house, but two ordinary citizens—may change the way we all travel in fifteen or twenty-five years.

I salute the imagination, creative ability, and the hard physical work required of all of these inventors as they searched for solutions to the world's problems. Everything starts out as just an idea in the imagination, and the biggest ideas are routinely rejected by the first people to hear them as impractical, impossible, not worth doing, or just out-and-out crazy: landing on the moon, building the Great Pyramids or the Panama Canal, D-day, you name it.

"It won't work." I hear that all the time. I *think* it all the time. Everyone is a critic. Who doesn't love to shoot down someone else's idea? Gosh, that's fun. The problem is, critics don't do things; creators and innovators do things. They change the world around them.

Everything starts with just an idea, and imagination changes everything.

Belief #20:
Ideas Come Anytime, Anywhere

Ideas come anytime, anywhere. So be ready, be open, and be looking for them. Try to record what occurs to you somehow: thoughts, questions, and observations, as well as fully formed product concepts. We are always looking for inspirations, insight, observations, or questions that might frame or inspire a new product direction.

Great discoveries and ideas have arrived as someone was dozing off at home or stepping onto the bus. Ideas can and do come at any time and from anywhere. Like a writer who pays close attention to the people and places he or she encounters, gathering source material for that next novel, we make it a habit to constantly scan the everyday world for objects, observations, trends, and devices that we can share with the team as a possible beginning of a new idea.

Invention, creativity, and innovation are everywhere. The inspiration for the next great idea in retailing, restaurants, hair styling—and yes, even toys and games—is all around us right now. As a famous thinker once said, "We stand on the shoulders of giants."

Any new thought we have is based on the thinking of those who came before us.

I love Cracker Barrel restaurants. You probably do, too, if you have ever had the pleasure. I always find cool toys in the adjoining general stores, and the food can always be counted on to be mouth-wateringly delicious. But if you ever pass by Sikeston, Missouri, don't miss a place called Lambert's Café, home of the "throwed rolls." They throw the rolls to you from across the restaurant, and they are too good to drop. The restaurant has a little general store and a very cluttered country motif that may seem a tad familiar. Lambert's Café, of Sikeston, Missouri, has to be the prototype for Cracker Barrel restaurants. There can be no doubt. Someone looking for a restaurant concept must have found this country classic and decided to clone it, or perhaps franchise it, just as Ray Kroc did long ago with the McDonald's restaurant concept.

Good, and even great, kernels of ideas are all around us. We need but to look. A great product idea can come also from a mere question or observation. We are not always looking for fully formed, thought-out, whole-cloth ideas.

"Can we get a doll to stand up from a seated position?" became *TMX Elmo*.

"Can we do something with electrolysis?" became our *Hydrogen-Powered Rocket System*.

"Can we do something with Billy the Bass?" became *Baby Go Boom*.

Asking questions such as, "Could a water rocket be turned into a water gun?" (which led to the invention of the Super Soaker, perhaps?) will result in tremendously successful products. (We didn't invent the Super Soaker, by the way—had the idea; rejected it as too expensive. Damn!)

Belief #21:
The Best Idea Meetings Come From Intense Concentration

Creativity is the practice of creating, or bringing something into being, and it often involves tangible skills. Imagination is conceiving of what to create, prior to using creative skills to realize what the imagination has envisioned.

In meetings to discuss ideas and generate new ones, I have found that the best creative output comes from a state of intense concentration: what I call getting into "The Zone." This "Zone" may well be the same as the one that athletes and others describe. It involves carefully following the thread of the conversation, making sure one's ideas are inserted into the mix where applicable, and being attuned to one's own ideas and imagery that come up as the conversation flows. "The Zone" is a high state of awareness of everything that is said and is happening around oneself as well as a keen awareness of the thoughts that spring to mind based on what is heard and seen in the meeting. It involves little evaluation—just imagining, capturing, and articulating ideas as they appear.

A good meeting needs flow. We look for an uncensored, quickly articulated flow of ideas, images, and thoughts. No one need be profound, but each idea offered can and will trigger ideas and thoughts in others if they are in the flow. Don't censor any ideas. Without disrupting the flow, get them into the meeting as soon as possible and where they are appropriate. Don't hold back. Actively listen and actively participate. Each thought voiced will create more in others and in the self, like a stone thrown into a pool of water.

Brainstorming sessions can work, but much of the time, they just don't. Ideation or brainstorming—whatever it is called—is a game with rules and needs an acquired expertise similar to any other sport, trade, or field of endeavor. Just showing up doesn't produce results. It is a team endeavor, and poor or unskilled effort from any one team member can keep the entire team from being successful. Just as in baseball, tug-of-war, or a canoe race, everyone has to give his or her best effort and, ideally, play at the same skill level and at the same high level of intensity.

Like success in anything, bringing focus, concentrating, attending to the rules of play, and desiring to succeed are key elements in getting results in ideation sessions. The larger the group, the more likely it is that players will vary greatly in level of focus and desire, and therefore the results will suffer. This is why I am a strong proponent of one-on-one idea sessions, as focus and concentration are almost always assured.

The structure of an idea meeting and the techniques used in it, not surprisingly, can have a tremendous impact on the quality of its results. One-on-one meetings work well because there are no distractions. We are forced to hang on the other person's every word, as it quickly becomes obvious when you aren't truly "there." Our cultural mores cause us to be better at paying attention when we are not part of a group, as seen in the "bystander effect" when someone is being attacked. Studies find that a lone person is far more likely to rush to help than the typical person in a group, who will expect someone else to rush in for them. This model is often evident in group idea sessions, where participants are comfortable with letting others do the work. It is human nature, but each meeting participant (this means you!) should try to force him or herself to participate actively and continuously.

Listening is key, but not the kind of listening you likely practice very often. Typical "listening" is often only waiting for another person to stop talking (shut up already!) so that we can say what we have been thinking of and want to say. We are unable to pay attention to what others are saying, for fear of forgetting what we want to say. Therefore, we aren't listening at all.

Active listening is not like everyday listening. It is a skill that can be developed and takes real work and effort to do continuously. Just because I know how to throw a ball doesn't make me a major-league pitcher. The difference between backyard catch and

World Series pitching is great. So it is with listening. We may well think we do it and that we know how, but what I am describing is another skill altogether.

A crucial component of creative listening is to be tuned into one's own ideas that spring to mind from what is being heard. Like a room full of mousetraps, tossing out an idea conjures up other ideas, and we want to make sure we capture and share these random thoughts. You must write them down so that they are not lost, but also so you can temporarily forget them and return to what the other group members may be saying. Jot down ideas as they occur so you can continue to be an attentive and active listener. Pay attention to your imagination.

Then you need to interject these thoughts, incomplete as they may be, while the relevant topic is still under discussion. Get them out and on the table right then, because they will be fodder for others' ideas in turn. Like the accretion of ice layers on a ball of hail, bit by bit, more and more thoughts can be added to an idea until a real, actionable concept is formed. If your thought is on another tangent and would derail the conversation rather than serve to elaborate or support it, then hold onto it and get it in as soon as the topic changes.

In any idea session, it is essential that you get your ideas into the mix, even if you feel you have to raise your hand to be acknowledged and heard. This was a problem for me as a young designer.

When describing your idea, be brief, be crystal clear, and be to the point. If there is little positive response, it is not likely that you were misunderstood, but rather that your peers lack interest or excitement in your idea. Let it go. You will find that little comes from trying to sell your concept or attempt to solicit greater interest through more explanation. If people want more explanation, they will ask.

Selling, or offering further explanation out of the assumption that people don't understand your idea, will frustrate the other participants (who are not dummies, by the way, or they wouldn't be there). It halts the flow of the meeting and kills the creative energy. Trying to "sell" your idea to the group is like teaching a pig to sing; you annoy the pig and frustrate yourself.

Whatever you do, if you want to come up with some good ideas, first you must come up with *lots* of them. Idea generation is a developable skill that requires practice and use, and a desire to improve. Exercise and develop your imagination, because imagination changes everything.

CHAPTER IV

BELIEF #22:

Commit Yourself To Greatness

Belief #23:
Take A Pledge To Always Do Better

I still recall getting my very special Yankee Doodle rocket launcher for Christmas one year. After playing with it a few times, my heart sank. This toy that I had wanted for so long was such a disappointment. This was my big Christmas gift! It launched a simple, spring-loaded rocket. That was it. I had been duped.

You and I—all of us—suffer when such products fill the store shelves, are promoted on TV, and ruin a child's play on some special day. It makes people think all toys are junk, and we know that is not true. Our industry creates great products, and too few people know that.

The toy industry can always do better. We should take a pledge to always do better. Every toy company, every ad agency, every retailer, every inventor and toy designer should make a pledge, just like the physicians' Hippocratic oath "to do no harm."

Put up your right hand and repeat after me: "I will make and sell no bad toys. I will endeavor to create products with great value to the consumer and user. I will devote all my efforts to developing toys and children's products that excite, delight, inspire, and entertain. So help me, Santa!"

Lund and Company's goal, and my personal mission, is to create great products that inspire and entertain. We strive for products that deliver great value to the consumer for the hard-earned money spent.

When I hear people complain about toys and the toy industry, I wince. There are many great toys on the market now, and wonderful new toys are introduced each year. No other industry delivers so much innovation so quickly and at such great value for the money as the toy industry. But, as an industry we are sometimes guilty of foisting crap onto the marketplace, as well. We all suffer when bad toys are TV promoted and flood the toy store shelves. I am not talking about cheaply made Chinese toys, but rather toys made and promoted by US-born-and-bred toy companies. It ought to be against the law.

What are the characteristics of a good toy, or even a GREAT toy? How many dimensions do we need to include in measuring greatness? The name of the product, the packaging, and the promotion, as well? We have created and licensed many successful products over the years; some of them were great, while others were perhaps only good. On the other hand, some products that our licensee, the client company, and the manufacturer recognized as very good—even great—were not successful in the marketplace. And then there are many products we created that I believe to be great toys and games, yet we have been unable to license them. They sit in our vault, underappreciated and uncommercialized. Even great products may also need great packaging, PR, and promotion to achieve success.

Belief #24:
Endeavor To Create Products With Great Play Value

What is a good toy? What is play value? What is interaction and interactivity in a toy? What is a truly turn-on "watch-me" toy that doesn't require interaction with the child, and what is not? Are there different types of play value and interaction that toys may have?

I think what makes a good toy is more easily answered than what makes one GREAT. But what separates good from great? There are many opinions on this. Some toy forms do not pass muster on a reviewer's spectrum of what is politically correct. It's like asking a question to which you already have an answer or doing a research project with a preconceived set of correct answers, as opposed to an honest search for the truth. For example, some reviewers won't allow toy guns on their lists of good or great toys, while others choose to eliminate one or another product category for their own personal reasons.

There was once a category of toys called airport toys, which were classic "watch-me" toys. Most often, a character of some sort would roll down an inclined track, be mechanically picked up at the bottom, and returned to the top of the track to roll down once more. These toys had no interaction, only a switch to turn them on so that you might watch them cycle over and over. These were truly "watch me" toys, and were thus arguably neither good nor great, though fun to watch. I don't see them in airports much anymore.

My question is really not what makes a toy good, but what makes a toy GREAT? If it has stood the test of time, does this mean it is great? Is there a formula, such as price vs. play? Does each dollar a toy costs correspond to the duration of time that a child will play with it? Let's consider a formula:

$$\text{Great} = \text{play hours/dollars (or } G = p/d)$$

The greater the value of G, the greater the product. Make sense?

If a doll costs \$8.00 and the child plays with it for 10 hours ($G = 10/8 = 1.25$), then G is greater than 1, and it is arguably a great toy. If the toy costs \$20 and the child plays with it for 2 hours ($G = 2/20 = .10$), then G is .1 and it is far less likely to be a great toy. It would be very interesting to know how many hours various types of toys are played with over their lifespan in a child's life. I suppose scientists might try and track toys, the way they do fish, geese and other wild life, to get at that over a toy's life span.

Great toys, by definition, have great play value. Think construction toys and building blocks, slot cars, die-cast vehicles, fashion dolls, balls, flying discs, and mechanical drawing toys. These toys involve almost constant hands-on contact by the child. Many of our products over the years have been of this type: highly interactive, hands-on play type toys, including our dolls *Baby Alive Sip 'n Slurp* by Hasbro and *Little Mommy Baby Knows* by Mattel. These both provided highly engaging, hands-on fun and were very successful as a result.

Watching someone play with *TMX Elmo*, you'll invariably see laughter. People can't wait to see what he does when you tickle him again. The fact that the user is engaged to the point of laughter suggests to me that this is a truly interactive toy, even though it does not have a constant, hands-on play pattern and is not physically interactive in the manner of some of the great toy categories I mentioned before. Yet there are others of the type where one pushes the button on the hand and watches the sequence that could arguably be defined as "watch-me" toys.

Belief #25:
Toys Should Excite, Delight, Entertain, And Inspire

My personal service goal is to enrich the lives of others through the products that we invent and license, and beyond that, to inspire others through play. I believe that some children will be so fascinated by one of our products that it will influence what they do as adults. It may encourage them to become engineers, inventors, artists, scientists, doctors, or pursue some other line of work in which they will make a contribution to the world. It will all have started with a toy, one of our creations. Toys delight, entertain, educate and inspire, and thus, toys change the world.

Not too long ago, I had the extreme pleasure of giving my yearly talk about my career as an entrepreneur, independent businessman, inventor, and specifically, a creator of toys and games, at a local school's Career Day. Through stories about *Fireball Island, VacMan, TMX Elmo, Baby Go Boom, Tumble Time Tigger,* and our *Talking Electronic Microscope,* I was able to share with those students my enthusiasm and passion for the process of invention.

Fireball Island was inspired by a 3-D, distortion-printed, vacuum-formed map that I envisioned as a great new type of game board surface, and it was. *Vac Man* was inspired by a photo in a book on pneumatic structures. The photo showed an example of a vacu-umatic arch that was soft, like a giant beanbag, until the air was evacuated and it formed into a rigid arch on which a person could sit. *Tumble Time Tigger* started life as a doll, and the original cartwheeling doll started life as a question: "Can we make a motorized, cart-wheeling doll?" It turned out, after many months of work, that we could indeed!

At the end of my presentation, the eighth-graders swarmed over *Vac Man*, pumping, stretching, and marveling at a little bit of magic they had never seen before. A group of girls took up playing with *TMX Elmo*, giggling, laughing, and having a wonderful time. Good toys excite and delight. It is too bad they have such a short life in the stores, because their appeal is enduring.

I love this work. I can't think of anything else I might enjoy doing. I love the processes of exploration, tinkering, and discovery. Every day, we encounter different challenges and opportunities. I hope that we can make a contribution to your life someday, if we haven't already, through our efforts to create wonderful new products that inspire, excite, and delight. And oh, make you laugh as well!

Belief #26:
Toy Stores Should Be More Entertaining And Fun

I love going into toy stores, particularly the little ma-and-pa stores, and I am always delighted to stumble upon them in my travels. I can't wait to get in and see what they have—to look at everything, touch everything, pick up, rattle, examine, and marvel at everything!

A good toy store is a riot of color, shape, texture, things that make sounds, things made of wood, plastic, or fur, with eye candy and finger candy everywhere. It is a little bit of Willy Wonka and Disney World just off the sidewalk and through the door.

A toy store is an entertainment destination, not just a shop for selling toys. If stores could capitalize on the entertainment facet of their business, if they could be more entertaining still, they would draw more customers in, like at FAO Schwarz, or the legendary Safe House in Milwaukee, where they have perfected the art of dining as entertainment.

I realize that operating a small toy store must be a hard row to hoe at times. Making a toy store more entertaining would cost money, but that investment might pay off many times over, and over, and over with an increase in visitors. More people will come, and surely more toys will be sold.

What can smaller toy stores do to capitalize on the entertainment value of the store as a destination? How can they make the space more entertaining, and therefore, draw more people in? Do you remember department store toy departments and sitting on Santa's lap as a child? I certainly do. I recall being heartbroken when Marshall Fields discontinued their magical toy department—a place of wonder that seemed as if it had been transported directly from Santa's North Pole complex, complete with Santa Claus himself (my boss and idol!).

No toy store today captures the magic of a department store toy department. Instead of shrinking their toy department, Walmart needs to make it a magical place, different from the laundry and bleach section, more wonderful than bedding and clothes. They could create several aisles of whimsy, magic, and wonder that the consumer would want to enter and dawdle in, remembering their childhoods and dreams of toys. And at the holidays, crank it up a notch on the wonder and whimsy scale. If Walmart wishes, we will gladly consult on this transformation! Cutting SKUs and cutting the toy department is not the way to serve customers—who all have children and grandchildren, nieces and nephews, that love to play with toys!

Who doesn't love to peruse the toy aisle in Walgreens and other drug stores? My heart leaps when I see an aisle of toys in a home supply store like Menards. Toys are fun, and it always gladdens my heart to see them on the store shelf—especially, by surprise, somewhere other than in a toy store or toy department.

There has never been more opportunity in retailing toys than today. Buy toys; they are an investment in joy and happiness. Every toy creates at least a mile of smiles, one face at a time. Toys are not like dishware or hand soap. Who has fond memories of pots and pans from their youth? Who has dreams of shampoos and fingernail brushes dancing around in their heads? No one does. But who does not have fond memories of childhood toys, and who has not had dreams of Christmas magic, Santa, toys, reindeer, and other holiday fantasies, like sugarplums dancing in their minds?

Toys are different. Toys are laden with powerful emotional content and context. For this reason, toys should not be merchandised like pots and pans and hand soap. To do so takes away from the magic and wonderment of the toys themselves, and prevents the consumer from referencing his or her own fond memories of toys, play, holidays, Christmas, and all the powerful emotions associated with these things. Retailers need to wake up to the opportunity to speak and market more directly to that part of the consumer psyche. Walmart and others are missing the essence of what toys are to all of us, and are missing sales and revenues as a result.

Walmart doesn't get it. Target doesn't get it. Toys are not being marketed properly. Toys are being under-marketed. Retailers do not acknowledge or take advantage of the power toys have over each of us to rekindle positive memories and emotions, particularly during holiday seasons.

What would it take to transform the toy department to a special place year-round, perhaps even a place of wonder and magic at the holidays? And what would be the payoff of that investment? It would be worth trying, even as an experiment, or on a trial basis. The investment could be small, but the payoff—HUGE! A win-win for retail, toy industry, and consumer.

Belief #27:
Be An Industry On A Mission

In 1992, we changed our company name from Lund and Company to Lund and Company Invention, LLC, to focus our collective minds on the fact that we are inventors, not just designers. As a result, we became better at what we do. We adopted as our mantra, our mission statement, "We bring small things to life," and in doing so we have achieved more and gotten better at just that. We looked toward where we wanted to go, and the change in our work followed naturally from it. Intentionally stating what we were and wanted to be has helped us as a team to be far better at each of our jobs.

The toy industry can create its own mantra, its own unique mission statement. It must be short, sweet, and powerful, and it must speak of the creation and marketing of great products that are safe and innovative and that inspire, delight, educate, and enrich the lives of others. We can remind the public that this is the kind of industry we are and that these are the kinds of products we are dedicated to creating. Each member company can put this pledge on all its packaging, like the Good Housekeeping Seal, and it will distinguish Toy Industry Association (TIA) toy companies from other toy marketers who do not subscribe to this high standard. We can visualize ourselves as a great industry that creates great products that are important to children and to our society as well. Envisioning ourselves as great will make us greater—perhaps greater by far than we might ever have believed possible.

The toy industry needs to promote the impact and importance of toys in society. Make toys important, not just a luxury or a nice-to-have, but as essential as food and water in the nurturing of the child. Toy retailers should take the lead on this. R U listening?

Toy companies need to innovate, invent, create, and bring to market powerfully compelling products at a great value. Toy companies need to market these products in ways that the consumer cannot ignore. We need masterful marketing, not the mundane and humdrum, and we need incredible, wonderful products that kids and consumers cannot resist.

The toy industry has taken a shellacking. Kids choose computer and video games and electronic gadgets over toys. Costly, high-profile safety recalls have given the toy industry a black eye, resulting in overreactions by legislators around the country. Commodity price swings have wreaked havoc with product costing, as have labor and electric power shortages in China. And thousands of Chinese toy factories are going out of business or just getting out of toys. We lost our own beloved toy building at Fifth Avenue and Broadway in Manhattan, and the New York toy district is no more. So it goes.

Toy companies, and the industry as a whole, need to learn how to deal with the next consumer safety crisis or other emergency with truly convincing remorse. Toy companies and the industry must act like responsible global corporate citizens in the way they clean up any future mess (at least one will surely come along). The Tylenol poisoning scare of long ago is an example of how a company stood up and cleaned up the mess in a way that no one could fault them.

Toys matter. No other industry brings more new products or so much innovation to market each year than the toy industry. No industry puts more feature and value into their product, at a better price, than the toy industry. On occasion, I hear people say, "there's nothing new or interesting in toys." The average person is unaware of all the new, interesting—and at times, amazing and revolutionary—new technologies and innovations embodied in toys.

Some of the very first electronic consumer products were toys and games, such as Milton Bradley's Starbird Intruder and Simon, or the Parker Brothers game Merlin. The first consumer product with electronic speech was a Milton Bradley game. Webkinz were an innovation in product connected to the web. Our *Hydrogen-Powered Rocket System* was an entirely new technology in the marketplace, not just in the toy aisle. If engineers were to look closely at some of our mechanisms, such as the one inside *TMX Elmo*, they might find mechanical solutions they have never seen before that could be adapted elsewhere. The toy industry is a source of constant innovation, but few report on it, and very few are even aware of it.

I maintain that no other category of product has such a profound influence on our future. We can be proud of what we do, and yet strive to always do better. We need to shine a bright light on this industry and its constant stream of fun, but also on the education and innovation that we bring to market each year, inspiring children and the adults that they become.

Here's my prescription for the toy industry: it should formulate a message to the public on the profound importance and impact of toys on children, and therefore the profound impact of toys and play on adults. Adults run the world, make discoveries, change society, influence politics and thinking, so toys impact our world more than any other product category. Frank Lloyd Wright and the Wright Brothers concur on the power of toys in their lives. *Toys matter!*

And retailers need to wake up and smell the peppermint candi caynes! (note: clever intentional misspelling to get your attention) Do not market toys in the boring manner in which you are currently doing. Make the toy department special and magical. If you can't do it, I will take a year off and do it for you—store by store, in Walmarts, Targets, and even Sears and Kmarts across the country.

Market to the part of the consumer's psyche for which toys still are magical and laden with powerful emotional content.

Belief #28:
Do It Or Forget About It

There is a lot of talk about New Year's resolutions, and their failure, every year. The concept of New Year's resolutions tarnishes the topic of goal setting by depicting it as a fruitless, probably futile effort, to be given a cursory attempt each January and then discarded. Rather, goal setting is a very powerful tool that we can all use. There are ways that work, and there are ways that do not. There are big, generalized goals and mission statements, and there are smaller, measurable, and more specific goals, too.

I am here to tell you that I have set goals that worked, and I have set many a goal that did not. The ones that worked were good, useful goals, but the ones that did not work were not well-framed goals. Garbage in, garbage out. Poor goal in, no results out. Good goal in, good results out.

Not so many years ago, I set a goal to be more involved in the toy industry rather than just criticize those who gave of their time and energy to run it. I resolved to be more involved and have a higher profile. As a part of that larger effort, I resolved to write a blog, and to my own amazement and delight, I have done it more or less regularly for a few years now. Some of you out there have actually read it, and at least one person appears to like it (I think).

When invited to write an article for a magazine or something like that, I do it. If I am invited to speak somewhere or to be interviewed, I do it. My efforts have improved our business in tangible and intangible ways. I feel that I am able to make more contributions to more people and to the industry. I have a mission to spread the word about the importance of toys in our society, our culture, our civilization, and our world. I take every opportunity I am given to spread that message. I am pleased to see myself continue to pursue this goal. It is not attainable once and for all, like running a marathon; rather, it is an ongoing mission.

Then there are things that are like goals, but are not goals, per se, as they were not premeditated and articulated desires, but desired results achieved nonetheless. We have made some decisions to change over the years that have had profound effects on our business. A while back, we articulated for ourselves the desire not just to create products and thereby make a living, but to create great products, the very best that we are able. This is a guiding mission more than a goal, but I see it working. Most recently, a new client came to us; they had canvassed the invention community and chose us for collaboration ahead of all the rest.

We set a true goal to build a new studio that would inspire me and my team to do the best work of our lives and to inspire others to want to work with us. We have achieved it. Our new offices inspire us, and those who visit are astounded and delighted by what they see. One's environment has a powerful impact on one's work and life.

Years ago, we changed the way we work. Rather than just make toys, we began to explore technologies in depth over a period of years. We now go "where no one has gone before," into uncharted waters where we find things truly new to the world, and create new product applications and new magic using old and familiar actions, mechanisms, and principles.

As on a motorcycle, we go where we look. I'm not sure how it works, but if we take our eyes off the road, we will end up off the road in no time at all. Goals and guiding missions are the road that we probably should keep our eyes on to get where we want to go. Doing so can have profound effects on the results we achieve and the lives we lead. And we are doing the best work of our lives, just as we have set out to do.

Belief #29:

Success And Failure Matter Less Than Just Doing It

After graduating from college, I got off the education and life track that I felt I had been on since kindergarten. Rather than continue on down the line in the expected manner to become a doctor, lawyer, or go to graduate school, I hopped off. I had just returned from a cross-country bicycle trip. "Carolina to California," read the backs of our shirts. I tried to get a job out in Berkeley, California, so that our travels might continue, but I was overeducated and unable to get a simple cashier or restaurant job.

I was to be the best man at a friend's wedding, so I hitchhiked home, back across the country. I was dismayed that I couldn't readily find work and that I had to buy my best friend some ordinary wedding gift. I decided to apprentice as a leather worker, and learn a trade with which I could support myself even if World War III were to occur, which back then seemed like a real possibility. I would be able to make gifts for friends and family rather than just buy them something at the store, and if disaster struck, I could make useful and necessary things that I could barter for food and other necessities. I was always thinking.

My apprenticeship was a seminal experience, one of the most significant in my life. I had my first real business and learned that I liked it. It set the tone for the rest of my life; I have mainly been self-employed since. "Make s%&* and sell it" became my mantra.

After a year, I took over the leatherworks store in Chapel Hill, North Carolina, so that Stu and Pam, the master craftspeople I worked for, could retire to the country for a spell. You know, a "put your feet up, set a spell" kind of spell. That's Southern for "a brief period," which, depending on context, may be as short as a few minutes; in this case, it was about a year!

My workshop was in Frog Level, North Carolina—just an intersection, really – and I stopped there each morning to finish up shoes or sandals, of which I made many hundreds of pairs. Each pair was custom made, custom fitted, and cobbled with tacks in the ancient style of shoe making. From Frog Level, I would drive to the tiny (I mean really small, maybe 150 square feet), second-floor store on Franklin Street, above the stereo shop and in front of the Second Hand Rose vintage clothing store, just off Chapel Hill's main street. All day I would make bags, belts, take custom orders, fit shoes and sandals, trace feet for new pairs, and sell the beautiful leather goods that Stu or I had made. I worked long and hard and loved every minute of it.

When Stu and Pam returned to their store after a year's break, I moved away so as not to compete, and began my sojourn and a new leather business in San Antonio, Texas. I set up shop in an un-air-conditioned, black-shingled garage, where I learned to sweat. And sweat I did. Summer is long and hot in south Texas. So are spring and fall.

Years later, with graduate school behind me and having apprenticed at Marvin Glass and Associates to learn the business of toy invention, I left the nest to begin on my own again. I consider myself unemployable and only suited to working for myself, so that's what I do.

When I turned sixty, I realized that the things I had long thought I would do one day, well, I had better start doing them, or just forget about it. I'm not getting any younger, better looking, or more energetic. Do it, or forget about it. Success doesn't matter. Doing things does.

I believe in doing, not so much in talking. For many years, I have clung dearly to the notion of retiring one day and opening a leather shop like I once had in some lakeside tourist town, college town, or similar. As time has passed, the idea of retiring has faded and the shop of my dreams has evolved from a quaint little leather shop to a leather-goods maker, to something more on the order of Coach. Lund Leather may one day become a brand known far and wide for high-quality, distinctive, beautiful, and functional art, all of the finest leather.

I got tired of hearing myself think about things, and decided to just do them. Success or failure does not matter. Doing it does. So I am. If you have a long-cherished dream, speak it, act on it, do it. Now or never. We have but one life to live, and it's not really all that long. Write the book, take up roller-skating, go diving, learn to dance, start the business. Success is less important than your attempts to realize your dreams.

My mother used to quote Tennyson's line, "Better to have loved and lost, than never to have loved at all." I would adjust it to "Better to have tried and failed than never to have tried at all."

CHAPTER V

BELIEF #30:

Teamwork Is Key To Doing The Impossible

Belief#31:
Teamwork Is Magic

Our best work by far is done as a team. Teamwork is invisible and is hard to identify, but like gravity and air, it is very real and very powerful. Teamwork is the magic that makes ordinary people able to do extraordinary things. Individually, we may not be all that remarkable (except to our parents, perhaps), but together we have the collective intellect and abilities of a genius! No one person could create the products we have invented over the years, but our talented team of hardworking designers, imbued with a generous spirit of collaboration, has been the source of many remarkable and remarkably successful toys.

We have been called the "masters of motion" and many consider us the best mechanism team in the industry. We have partnered with each other, and very importantly, we have teamed up with our clients, too. They have often challenged us to go beyond what even we believed was possible. We didn't always work as a team, but once we discovered the power of teamwork, and were able to encourage and sustain it, our work was transformed. Teamwork is magic. Teamwork is the key to our success. Teamwork makes the impossible possible.

Impossible is merely a concept—and most often only an opinion—rather than an "intersubjectively testifiable observation," aka, a fact. It is possible to accomplish the impossible once one believes something *is*, in fact, possible. Does that make sense? Believing something to be impossible makes it so. We choose to categorize certain things as impossible, and thus we make it true for ourselves. Not for others, just for ourselves.

Conversely, setting aside a belief that something is impossible, and acting as if it *were* possible, makes it possible. We once had a doll that could do cartwheels, and Fisher-Price asked if we could make a plush animal version: a Tigger character. We thought, "probably not," as the weight and thickness of the plush would interfere with the movement and it would not translate. But we gave it a try, and our team made it work, much to my surprise. The end result was *Tumble Time Tigger*—a successful and award-winning product.

Perfecting the mechanism was a big project and we encountered electronics problems that the designer on the project thought were impossible to solve. Because he was convinced it couldn't be solved, he could not solve it. It took another electronics expert to solve that problem. Once we had perfected the cartwheeling plush mechanism, we breathed a great collective sigh of relief and enjoyed a moment of triumph...until Fisher-Price told us to be "shelf-demonstrable," the Tigger would also have to do a cartwheel in the package! Surely *this* was impossible. It couldn't be done unless the package was six feet long! No way. But if the product was to go to market, it would have to do a cartwheel in the box. We set about solving the problem. With Tigger suspended in the box from a pivot on his back, we successfully made him do a cartwheel in the package. The end result was a breakthrough in on-shelf package design.

We have learned that we can indeed do the impossible if we set aside any preconceived notion that some desirable end result can't be achieved. Setting aside that belief makes the impossible become possible. It sounds like circular, tautological logic, but it is a simple concept, and true.

When we worked with Fisher-Price to develop the mechanism that became *TMX Elmo*, they wanted us to add an arm action and to accomplish all actions with only two motors. We were convinced that it was impossible and would require at least a three-motor mechanism. Then we set aside our disbelief and went about the task of doing just what they wanted. It was not easy, and some spectacular teamwork was required between designer, model maker, and electronics expert, but we did it. I believe the end result is one of the most elegant mechanisms ever used in a toy. We are very proud of it to this day.

TMX Elmo, as you may know, sold more units on the first day than any other toy in history. It was recognized by the TIA as the Preschool Toy of the Year and the Overall Toy of the Year in 2007. It brought smiles and laughter to tens of millions of people, if not more! So we continue our work, seeking to do what others might think cannot be done.

We love doing the impossible, because we know that if we succeed, no one will have done it before us—because they would not even have attempted it. We are pushing the envelope of mechanisms and mechanical technologies, and are attempting to do things with age-old phenomena that are entirely new to the world. I love what we do. We face different challenges every day, some so hard that they seem impossible—and we love that.

Belief #32:
Collaborate To Greatness

We all put our pants on one leg at a time, but when we put our heads together, collectively we have the brainpower of a genius. We see this time and again when we work in close collaboration as a team internally, as well as when we work hand in hand with our client companies. The best products come out of this teamwork. *TMX Elmo, Tumble Time Tigger,* and the *Hydrogen-Powered Rocket System* are all products that came to market as the result of close and often intense collaboration.

The toy industry can collaborate its way to greatness. Collaborate with consumers, collaborate with inventors, collaborate with retailers. Collaborate and innovate! If you make it great, they will come! Retailers will *have to have* these products on their shelves, because consumers will be looking for them. Now, I am a product guy, and a great product is part of the collaboration to greatness. But genius-level marketing will be equally important.

As an industry, we are undershooting our potential and letting our business be taken away from us. That would be a disservice to children and to the world at large. For children, toys are bigger and more important than mere playthings. Toys inspire, educate, and fascinate our young, and as a result, toys are engines of cultural innovation, progress, discovery, and change. Play is important business! *Toys matter.*

Belief #33:
The Hallmark Of Teamwork Is Generosity Of Spirit

We once finished a big project with great team effort, whose end result was a fabulous, wonderful toy. The products were mechanical and the mechanisms were precisely controlled by electronics, and we needed scripting and play patterns that would make them engaging and fun to play with. Their development required the time and talents of several people. Individually, we are ordinary, but together we can be extraordinary.

I have seen the power of teamwork again and again. It is invisible to the naked eye, tasteless, and transparent, but very real, and extraordinarily powerful. It is hard to define, but you will know when it is there. Teamwork yields results not possible by any other means.

One hallmark of teamwork is a generosity of spirit: a willingness to help the team, however and whenever needed. I can recall a crystal-clear example when once, on a Friday afternoon, part of our team was continuing work on a product that would likely go into the evening and through the weekend. Another team member, whose talents were not essential at that stage of the project, stopped to ask that the team call him in anytime over the weekend if his assistance would be helpful. That is teamwork.

Together, we create products that amaze and delight, including some that didn't seem possible at the outset. Teamwork produces miracles. You can't buy it or acquire it. It must be created and nurtured. Your greatest results will come from teamwork.

Belief #34:
Don't Ever Forget The Value Of Respect

No team can survive if its members don't value and protect a positive, respectful workplace environment. In any organization, courtesy and respect is the oil that lubricates the contact between individuals who work together like meshing gears. When workers do not treat each other with respect, problems arise, feelings get hurt, resentments fester, and the work of the entire group suffers the consequences. Such a group cannot function as a team.

The boss, supervisor, or owner has a responsibility to provide an environment that allows and encourages respect among colleagues and associates. That would be me. Over the past twenty-five years, I hope that I have improved in this aspect of my role as captain of the ship, human resources manager, and chief cook and bottle washer. But there is always need for improvement, in all things. Always seek to improve.

The team members, conversely, have a responsibility to bring concerns to light as they arise, and not allow them to devolve into problems. Big kudos to those team members who can do just that. It takes courage and a proactive attitude to bring a problem up to the boss, supervisor, or owner that they would rather not hear about.

A team is like a family. Everyone in it is a unique individual, with individual goals, needs, agenda, ego, sensitivities, and insecurities. Like a family, to create a positive environment for ourselves, we need to treat others with love, kindness, and courtesy. We seek to be treated in kind, yielding the greatest level of happiness for all and the greatest results from the team.

In short, we get out of an environment what we put into it. Sorry, but it's true. Overused and trite? Maybe, but spot on. Give it your best, and you will get a lot of good back. Treat others with discourtesy or a lack of respect, and you yourself will suffer as a result. The way we behave comes back at us. If we treat others badly we do not make ourselves happy, but we create an unhappy environment in which we have to continue to live or work. Trust me: been there, done that, got the psychological bruises to show for it. Our behavior creates our environment. We are responsible for the environment in which we work because we create it. A great work environment allows great work.

Like other behaviors, courtesy to others can be as a pebble thrown into a pond of still water, causing ripples that spread out through space and time. At my fortieth high school reunion, a former classmate, who had long since slipped from my memory, recounted a story from our senior year. We had taken her father's pickup truck, without permission, to collect wood for a big bonfire at the high school. She recounted that her father had waited for us, and that on our return, I had stepped out of his truck and extended my hand to introduce myself and thank him for its use. A small, unremarkable moment it might seem. Yet, forty years later, her father still remembered me and that moment. So memorable was it that, over the years, he would inquire after me on occasion.

Another time, while hitchhiking from California back to my hometown in western New York, I was let off at some desolate, desert interstate exit in Nevada, joining a long string of hitchhikers who were there ahead of me with hopeful thumbs out seeking a ride! I joined the end of the line with a handwritten sign saying one word: "PLEASE." And wonder of wonders, I was the first to be picked up. That ride took me all the way to Pennsylvania—almost the entire way home. Courtesy works, if you ask me. (And, by the way, my new friend picked me up in a '50s vintage car nursed along at 55 mph, back when speed limits of 75 were common. Most traveled faster than that, of course, on the vast reaches of interstate concrete from Nevada across the Great Prairie. So, needless to say, it took a long time to get to PA! I ran out of money, subsisting on peanut butter, a loaf of bread, and a bag of apricots procured along the way. Haven't been able to eat apricots since.)

Courtesy is very powerful.

Belief #35:
Extraordinary Effort Yields Extraordinary Results

Extraordinary results come from extraordinary effort. It seems obvious that the world would work that way, but how many of us expect extraordinary results from ordinary effort? If you work a minimum number of hours, you might expect a minimum level of results. Why would anyone expect more?

It is hard to be more creative. I'm not sure how to be smarter. I don't think I can work any harder than I already do, or somehow get more done in the same amount of time! I have no idea how to get luckier. But I sure can put in more hours, above and beyond the minimum. And at least to a point, I can be fairly sure that this will yield greater results, all else being equal.

When we created the mechanism for our cart-wheeling *Tumble Time Tigger*, many a long day, an evening, and a weekend were spent in the quest to perfect it. The result was an extraordinary product. When we created the mechanism, actions, and play patterns for *TMX Elmo, TMX Cookie, and TMX Ernie*, our team worked many extra days, nights, and weekends meeting, tinkering, testing and experimenting tirelessly (and sometimes tiredly). It was a process of hard work and harder thinking, and the results speak for themselves.

Belief #36:
Persistence Succeeds Above All Else

Good times follow bad as surely as day follows night, in life and in business. We have known both on more than one occasion. In our early years, we rode high on the back-to-back successes of Milton Bradley's *Fireball Island* (now considered a cult classic, I've been told), *Baby Alive Sip 'n Slurp, Vac Man,* and our *Luminator Light-Up Sports Balls.* Each sold millions of units, and every year we doubled our revenues. I thought it would go up and up forever…until it didn't. We soon began a multi-year slide down the bell curve, which we barely survived.

The secret of success is never quitting. The secret of staying in business is, well, actually, just staying in business. Persistence. To paraphrase Rocky in his last movie, "it's not how hard you can hit, but how many times you can take a hit and get back up." Persistence overcomes all things. And by the way, overnight success takes twenty years! Sorry.

When we hit bottom the first time, we quit thinking about how good we were, how successful, how clever, or how inventive. We quit thinking that toy companies were idiots for not licensing our products. Instead, we started focusing on creating better products that the companies we work with actually wanted. We were not artists trying to please only ourselves, but in business, providing a product that answered someone's need. It felt like turning around a big ship at sea, and turning our ship around took years. But slowly, we did it. We created better products, and we began to enjoy greater success once more.

Long, Long ago, Steve D. at Hasbro gave me some of the best advice I ever received: "If you don't start showing us the kinds of products we are looking for, we are going to quit meeting with you." They were hard words to hear. Unvarnished truth is a rare and precious thing. I took it to heart. Thank you, Steve. We started listening, and the first fruit was our most successful baby doll ever: *Baby Alive Sip 'n Slurp!*

On a cross-country bicycle ride from Carolina to California (thirty-five hundred miles in thirty-eight days!) many summers ago, an old-timer in the mountains of Virginia told us "You can't get there from here." I've never had much patience for naysayers. It took persistence to get up and ride over a hundred miles every day into a relentless headwind, across vast plains, desert valleys, and mountain range after mountain range. And eventually, we got there! I think I learned a little about persistence and what can be done simply by trying and not giving up.

I know about not trying as well, and its consequences. After high school, I wanted to go to the Naval Academy in Annapolis to be a navy officer and follow in the footsteps of my dad, who had served aboard a ship in World War II and again in the Korean conflict. I didn't believe I could get an appointment from my congressman. Why ever would he pick me? So I didn't try—and guess what? I didn't go to Annapolis. I took an alternate route and became a naval midshipman. I found the navy was not my calling and was honorably discharged. Didn't believe, didn't try, didn't get what I wanted. As I look back, I have no regrets – but sometimes I do wish I had stayed around long enough to fly jets off the pitching deck of an aircraft in the middle of the night in the middle of the Indian Ocean.

I am a big believer in the power of persistence. I may not be as smart as some or as clever as others, but what I lack in the brains department, I make up by hard work and persistence. As the wind and water wear down the rock over time, persistence overcomes all things.

In our research and development process, we come up with many stand-alone products such as our games *Fireball Island* and *Dizzy Dryer*, or dolls such as *Baby Alive Sip 'n Slurp*. But we also engage in long-term exploration of technologies that intrigue us and that we believe have potential in toys. Researching a technology takes years, with many directions and applications explored. This persistence leads to discoveries, going "where no one has gone before," and the creation of truly new and innovative products.

Baby Go Boom, inspired by Billy the Bass, began a five-year exploration of a motorized hinge mechanism that, used in different ways and in combination with other mechanisms, led to many products that eventually came to market. These included *Somersault Sarah, Tumble Time Tigger, Get Up n Bounce Tigger,* and *Hop Along Katie.* (Other products of the research did not make it to market.) The culmination of our years of investigation into this hinge was the elegantly simple mechanism found in *TMX Elmo* and the *TMX Friends Cookie* and *Ernie.* It is primarily a one-motor hinge, but it is capable of doing more than any comparable toy mechanism ever.

Belief #37:
Pursue The Path To Constant Improvement

The one thing I know for sure is that the only constant is change. Change makes the world ever new, constantly fascinating, and ever challenging. All of the great toy companies of my childhood are history, and many are long gone: Remco, Matchbox, Topper Toys, Marx, Ideal, and others. I played with their toys for endless hours and days on end.

Most of the great toy companies that I worked with when I first started in this business are gone as well—gobbled up by larger fish in the sea, or just out of business: Lakeside, Schaper, Gabriel, Tonka, Kenner, Parker Brothers, Tiger Electronics, Milton Bradley, and Tyco. Many exist now only as brand names inside of Hasbro or Mattel. The lifespan of the average corporation is forty years.

The world is changing, the market is changing, the laws and regulations are changing, the companies we work with are changing in how they manage their businesses, and we must change along with all of it. Constant change leads to constant improvement. If it were easy, everyone would be doing it.

When I was contemplating retiring and returning to leatherwork, I thought I'd be spending my later days making beautiful things of the finest leathers in the world: handbags, luggage, attachés, garments, and sculpture. Or I could rent out boats and jet skis in Pompano Beach, and spend my days in shorts—without a shirt, but with a good tan. But then it occurred to me that at this point in my career, I am better now at what I do than I have ever been. I am more knowledgeable and better connected, and my team's skills are more highly developed. We are inventing and developing better products than ever before. Now is not the time to quit! Now is the time to put the pedal to the metal and put to use my gifts, knowledge, and abilities to the greatest extent that I can, and to do the best work of my life. My friend Reuben Klamer, inventor of the Game of Life, is still inventing well into his eighties!

With persistence and perspiration, over time we improve at what we do. I am amazed when I look back and see how much better our products are now compared to only five years ago. Year by year, we get constantly better. We have to, or we would be out of business.

At this stage of my life, I am physically stronger than I have ever been. From years of weight training, I am now lifting weights I would have never imagined, and setting personal bests continuously—all at a time when I really expected that the best I could do would be to maintain strength, not increase it. If we make constant improvement a goal, we will constantly improve. We can get better, faster, stronger, and smarter at what we do if we strive to do just that. If we are to survive in business, this is imperative.

It is important to me to realize that this principle applies in my life, as well. I *can* get healthier, stronger, more loving, and better in my relationships with those around me. I don't have to ever stop improving in each and every aspect of my life. One day, back when I was thinking I was getting old, I was at my local motorcycle dealership. I met a rider who was eighty-five. He had just stopped riding two-up with his wife on back. He was just beginning to think of getting a three-wheeler or trike. To him, I was just a kid. And so, a kid I will be until *I* am eighty-five!

Be the best you can be, and then keep getting better. You are not old until you're dead. Go out each day and do the very best you can, and then do it again tomorrow. To do less is to waste the gift of life you have been given.

There have been athletes who have approached perfection in almost every field. Thomas Edison did so as an inventor, and Gandhi did so as a leader and a human being. The Safe House in Milwaukee, the coolest restaurant/bar in the world, is perfection. In my opinion, not one thing could be done, improved, or removed to make it more perfect! Chicago's Arun's restaurant, a five-star eatery, is Thai food perfection. Its stars are well earned. Margie's Candies, a Chicago destination for sports stars, the Beatles when they visited our fair city, and for the Mayor and his guests (including at least two presidents), is another quite different form of perfection.

When we aspire to perfection, we stay on a path of constant improvement, which survival in business and success in life require. The quest for perfection yields worthwhile results, regardless of how short we may fall.

CHAPTER VI

BELIEF #38:

═══════

This Is Your Life:
Live It And Love It

Belief #39:
Put The Pedal To The Metal

I like to drive. For the Super Bowl one year, I drove from Chicago to Miami and back in a three-day period. I mean, I drove all twenty-two-plus hours straight, even through an ice storm that shut down the interstate, while my fellow travelers slept much of the way. We spent one day there and drove back the next, amounting to forty-eight hours of driving in a seventy-two hour period. Crazy? Perhaps!

The next weekend, I drove from Chicago to southern Missouri and back—twice. And again, I drove straight into the worst ice storm they had ever seen down there. All the power was out when I got there, so we had to leave and come back a day later. That was a long weekend and a lot of miles.

I guess I am a driving fool. I have always loved road trips. I've bicycled, driven, and hitchhiked across the country, and I've motorcycled around all five of the Great Lakes, the Blue Ridge Parkway, to Sturgis, to LA, and elsewhere.

Driving is a metaphor for the way I live my life and my approach to the work that I do. I put the pedal to the metal and pride myself on having endurance and persistence beyond reason. Life is to be lived in the extreme, not to be taken easy. I don't do "laid back" real well. My approach to business, invention, family, motorcycling, driving, and life are all the same: foot to the floor, highballing like a southbound train, not to be stopped, deterred, or slowed down. Life is too short.

Life is to be lived—not just walked through, but savored. The bitter and the sweet, the salty, the savory, and the sour: each is a flavor of life, and they are all different, just as each course of a meal is not a sweet dessert. Each texture and flavor may be savored as a part of this meal called life that has been put before us.

Belief #40:

The Secret To A Happy Life Is Simple

Not easy, perhaps; but simple:

- Free your heart from hatred

- Free your mind from worries

- Live simply

- Give more

- Expect less.

Children are masters of the art of play—and how to live life! They simply know how to do it better than anyone else. They innately know how to create entertaining fun out of anything: the proverbial cardboard box, water, a stick, stones, and as I have witnessed once, mud.

At a birthday party once, I watched middle schoolers play, throwing water balloons, then dousing each other with buckets of water, ultimately creating a mud pit in the yard. The mud then became the toy. They smeared it all over themselves and each other, and threw mud balls until they were all covered in mud from head to toe. It was unbelievable to watch. It was crazy, insane fun and those kids will likely never forget that party. It was like Woodstock in the back yard! Kids know how to live life fully, how to play and experience joy. As adults we lose this.

When I was young, I had grass stains on the knees of my pants all the time. As an adult, the only way I get dirty is if I fall down, which is to say, almost never. What a shame that we give up play to such an extent as we get older. It is amazing to watch kids play. We adults, we have a lot to learn from them. I suppose everything that we know about creating toys and games comes from recalling our own play as children, or watching the play of others.

The mud pit party is an example of kids living large. But if that had been my yard and my party, I would never have let it happen. It would ruin the grass and ruin their clothes. What are the neighbors and the kids' parents going to think? While these are good questions and no one would disagree with the logic of this line of thought, it would still be wrong.

Grass can be reseeded and the yard repaired. Clothes can be washed, and who cares about the neighbors? I wouldn't have let the mud-fight happen, and I would have been wrong. Those kids played, they lived large, they had a time they will remember for the rest of their lives, and I got to see it. Conventional wisdom would have squelched it. I would have. It was crazy—out of bounds—and that is why it was so great.

There were times in my life when I might have been described as living large, and in other years, not so much. However, I intend to live large for the rest of the years I have. I intend to play every chance I get.

Everything begins with a yes. Nothing begins, nothing happens from the word no.

I have taken up roller-skating and find that I love it. I began with great trepidation about falling, breaking bones, and so on. After all, I am not eighteen years old any longer. But I survived and thrived. It was only a few years ago that I took up karate again after a twenty-five-year layoff. I ended up ruining my big toe joint while breaking boards with a front kick. Still, no regrets.

Around the same time, I took up tennis again after thirty years off. Both tennis and karate had been earlier passions at different times. After feeling a tear in my bicep while playing one day several years ago, I didn't have the sense to stop, and on the next swing I felt a bicep muscle rolling up in my arm like a window shade. (Some people don't have the sense the Good Lord gave a goose!) And still, I have no regrets—just one funny-looking "Popeye" bicep.

Belief #41:
The Meaning Of Life Is To Be Important In The Lives Of Others

I realized years ago that the meaning of life is to make a positive difference in the lives of others. This works for me, though you may have a different answer. As humans, we have an innate desire to leave our footprint behind, some mark by which others will know we were here, once upon a time. We hope to leave something of ourselves behind: children, in many cases, or just the change we effected, the contribution we made to the world. In my case, it is a body of work: the toys, games, and other products I have been a part of inventing and developing.

I am reminded again of my first mentor in the toy business, Harry Disko, now gone to greener pastures, but once Marvin Glass's right-hand man. He started on the bench as a model maker. Legend has it that on his first day, he found the shop too messy for his taste and took it upon himself to clean it. From that day on, he made sure that the model shop stayed clean and neat, just the way he liked it. Keeping the shop clean was not his job, but Harry was one to mold the world around him to his liking and to the benefit of everyone else, as well. He ultimately took over managing the business and proverbial heavy lifting, allowing Marvin to be the flamboyant, celebrity inventor loved by all. Marvin would give out compliments and raises. Harry would come along behind and rescind the raises, but the "atta-boys" and kudos the workers got to keep. Marvin did the hiring. Harry did the firing. He didn't mind getting his hands dirty. He ran a tight ship.

Harry gave me my first and only real job. He believed in me enough to give me a chance, and that has made all the difference to me. Thank you, Harry, wherever you are. I hope heaven is full of racetracks and raspberry patches.

For me, life and the work that we do is about service. I seek to serve my family and those close to me, and through our work creating new toys, games, and technologies, to serve children and their families around the world. For me, to serve others is the greatest gift; to serve my friends, especially in their times of need, to serve my children and family, to serve my amazing colleagues at Lund and Company Invention, and to serve the children of the world through the fruits of our thoughts and labor. To serve them all gives meaning to life.

Someone who made a difference in my life was Rob O., my high school tennis coach. He was an eccentric, former Canadian Junior Champion. He made me the number one singles star of our school, and no doubt a heartthrob for countless female classmates (in my dreams only, of course!). He would stand behind our opponents and jingle keys and coins in his pocket to distract them at key points in the matches, among many tricks he had up his sleeve. It didn't help. I still lost. Tennis was my passion in high school and he was quite a character. Still, he was my coach.

Another person who made a difference in my life was my sixth grade teacher Mr. M. I was saddened to learn of the recent passing of Mr. M. He had the famous "meatball row" in the back of the class for class clowns and ne'er-do-wells, from which I narrowly escaped being relegated. He had vivid stories of his Army experiences and high expectations of his students. I have never forgotten my time in his class. Mr. O. and Mr. M, wherever you are, thank you for all you have given to me and countless others before and since.

Teachers, parents, friends, and colleagues all touch the lives of so many others. Each day, we have opportunities to have a positive impact on others' lives if we look for them. To me, it is the greatest privilege to be important in the lives of others. There is no greater calling here on earth. It is a shame, perhaps, that we are too blithely unaware of our own importance in the lives of others and unappreciative of their importance in ours.

Belief #42:
Humans Are Hardwired For Giving

- Doing Good Feels Good

- Doing Good Can be Easy

- Each "yes" can make a difference in the lives of many

Do you know the feeling you get when you help a little old lady across the street? Feels good, doesn't it? (Except that one time at Toy Fair years ago, when I helped an elderly woman across Broadway and Fifth Avenue in New York. She started talking dirty to me and wanted me to go home with her! That was weird. But of course, it was New York. And I didn't.) There is something about doing a good deed that creates a special feeling of peace and satisfaction. I think we are hardwired for giving. We help others because others have helped us at times in our lives when we needed it. What goes around comes around; by giving and helping, we encourage the cycle of good deeds and generosity of others that we in turn benefit from. Keep it up.

I am very thankful for innumerable blessings and great good fortune. Happiness in life starts with a grateful heart. Many years ago, I sat next to a young woman, who was probably going to Toy Fair, on a flight to New York City. She told me a story of generosity and grassroots humanitarianism that I have never forgotten.

She had purchased a really nice pair of leather gloves for her brother for his birthday, around Thanksgiving, and for some reason had to return them. They had been fairly expensive. Before she left the store with the money, she went to the legendary Filene's Basement, where she saw a table of Day-Glo orange gloves on sale for $1 a pair. Of course they were cheap, because who wants Day-Glo orange gloves in the middle of the city? They are good for duck or deer hunting, maybe, so you don't end up getting stuffed and mounted. But in the middle of Boston or New York? Not so much.

So, the woman from the plane took the $40 from returning the pair of leather gloves and bought dozens of pairs of $1 Day-Glo orange gloves. She then distributed these gloves to the city's homeless, person by person, pair by pair, face to face. Many months later, she was gratified to see homeless people on the street still wearing Day-Glo orange gloves to warm their hands in the cold of winter.

I was struck by the way one woman, all on her own, bravely approached the untouchables of our society and touched the lives of so many in a meaningful way. She didn't spend a lot of money, or invest a lot of her time. It struck me that any one of us on any given day might be able to do something to bring comfort to others in need, one on one, or by the dozen as she had done. She was a grassroots, seat-of-the-pants humanitarian, and she set an example for me that I have never forgotten.

Belief #43:
Relish The Past, But Embrace The New

You've got two choices in life. Love it or hate it. Be happy or be miserable: you decide. No one else gives a rat's ass (with the possible exception of your mother. And please pardon the vernacular).

When I moved to Chicago over thirty years ago, I just knew I would hate living in a big city. So I did. I was miserable until I got over my self-generated conviction. Letting it go, I was able to embrace Chicago, explore it, and come to love the greatest city on earth.

When I lived in Texas, I knew many transplanted easterners who hated it. But I embraced the food and the culture, and loved it. Those who could not were miserable. It was their choice, and it was a bad one.

As an apprentice leatherworker, I was forced to listen to country music all day, every day, as we worked and sweated in the summer heat of Durham, North Carolina. Slowly, I began to know the songs and the singers, to appreciate the stories they told and the rich history of the individual artists, the music, and the traditions. I came to love country music once I was able to give up hating and rejecting it. It is truly wonderful, like Russian literature: an acquired but rewarding taste. Give it a chance; you may come to love it, too.

As a Dad, driving with my kids, I have been forced to listen to hip-hop and rap, which are supposed to be anathema to a middle-aged white male like *moi*—and to my astonishment, I have come to love them. They contain wonderful stories, humor, rhythm, and innovative sound—simply amazing. Like anything and everything else, much of the music is mediocre; a bit is pure dreck, but some is truly inspired. It is probably the most innovative and interesting music genre today. When you can be open to change or to the new, happiness is easier to achieve.

In the pursuit of happiness, we sometimes just have to get out of our own way. To sit back and judge is to distance and estrange ourselves from a musical genre, a religion, or a race of people; from family, friends, coworkers, and acquaintances; and estrangement leads to unhappiness.

Belief #44:
Visualize What You Seek

One day, while ventilating some solvent fumes out of the house, I was concerned about all the flies and dadgum mosquitoes that might also get in through the open doors. To keep things out, I went to close the garage door. As it started down, I thought, "Perhaps I should leave it open about six inches to allow air movement but minimize the bugs."

About six inches from the floor, the automatic garage door suddenly stopped. Did it hit something? I looked and found nothing interfering with the door or the electronic sensor. I tried the controls again: nothing; dead. After puzzling over this for a bit, I finally got out a ladder and checked the motor unit of the garage door opener, only to find that the electric plug had loosened itself just enough from the ceiling outlet to stop the door six inches from the bottom, exactly as I had been visualizing. That was curious. The plug had wiggled itself out of the outlet over years of use, just enough to cut power to the unit at precisely the moment I was considering stopping the door at that exact spot!

That is a trivial example of the power visualization has to affect the world around us. Visualize what you want; put out of your mind what you fear. Visualize happiness, visualize success, visualize whirled peas. (Bad joke.)

What you visualize will come to pass. Trust me on this. And if it doesn't, then what have you lost? What has it cost? Visualize and imagine all that you seek, every dream you would have come true, and avoid focusing on what you do not wish to happen.

Belief #45:
Look For The Good In People And In Life, And You Will Find It

Happiness hinges on our being thankful, I believe. Being thankful is to acknowledge all the great gifts bestowed upon us that we take for "granite" all the time. I am thankful for the gift of sight, of hearing, and the other senses that humankind seems to value only when it loses them. I am thankful for the gift of legs, arms, feet, and fingers—for the gift of life itself, to walk the earth, to breathe the air, to feel the sun, rain, and snowflakes on my skin. What great gifts these are.

I love being alive for this time that I have been allotted. I step out of the house on many a morning, breathe deep the air, and send up a prayer of thanks just to be here, to see the leaves change color and fall to the ground, to walk in the cool air, to contemplate a day of satisfying work ahead of me.

I am thankful to be able to love and be loved by my family and friends. I am thankful to be able to ride a motorcycle, to make things out of leather, to create and invent toys and things, to have learned to roller-skate so late in life. For all the years I have lived and all the experiences I have had, I am grateful.

If one cannot be thankful, one cannot be happy. If we are not thankful, then we are in danger of dwelling on not being tall enough, not being as good looking as some, not being as rich as others, or as successful, or famous, not having as big a house, or car, or…

I choose to be grateful again and again. It is a choice we can all make, and it needs to be made again and again, because as the vicissitudes (I love that word) of life wash over us like waves, it is easy to be knocked off balance and get caught up in dissatisfaction. We are here for but a blink of an eye.

Our time is short. In that time we have the opportunity to make a contribution to the world and to the lives of others. Now is our moment to breathe deep the smells and tastes, the tickles and touches, all the sensations and the gamut of emotions that life offers us each day, week, month, and year. The good and bad, happy and sad, the warm, the cold, the wet, and the dry. Ah, life is so delicious. I am thankful!

CHAPTER VII

BELIEF #46:

===

Don't Be Afraid To Fly

Belief #47:

Invention And Creation Require Great Courage

Innovation is all around us, all the time. I am astounded by the innovation that comes out of small-town farms, such as the original Big Foot vehicle (and from that, the world of Monster Trucks). It springs up out of urban neighborhoods, giving us pop locking, break dancing, hip-hop, rap, and low-rider cars. It is the destiny of humankind to create the new out of the old—to modify, extend, distort, add to or take away from, and recombine to create something new to the world, be it a song, a dance, a vehicle or—a dog.

On a five-thousand-mile road trip through New England to Nova Scotia (New Scotland), I encountered a dog species that had been "invented" (we might say *bred*) in the town of Yarborough, Nova Scotia. The little-known Duck Toller breed (it was certainly unknown to me, though you may be quite aware of it, world-wise and well-read as you are) looks a bit like a Collie; duck hunters use it to attract ducks. The Duck Toller dog performs a dance, and the ducks, apparently, come from all over to see what the heck that dog is doing. Then they are shot. It doesn't quite seem fair if you are a duck, but it is a stroke of genius if you are a duck hunter! Everything depends on your point of view, doesn't it?

I find it quite un-freakin'-believable that a dog can attract ducks, and even more so that long ago, someone in Yarborough, Nova Scotia, saw something in the original progenitor of the breed that they felt should be preserved and bred into dogs to attracts ducks to their untimely end. That is how one invents a dog.

What an idea. Surely, the dog inventor's friends and family must have said he or she was nuts when they heard about the plan to create a new dog species. Surely the creators of the great pyramids of Egypt, the Eiffel Tower, or the Suez Canal had to endure the doubts and even scorn of their spouses, families, and peers for contemplating their crazy notions. There are a million good reasons not to do something and only a few reasons at the outset to risk it all to do it anyway. But out of such crazy notions, great things arise. Case in point: modern civilization in all its forms and formats.

Innovation, invention, and creation require a certain type of courage: the courage to be wrong and the courage to embrace failure. Success may be found on this path and the world forever changed, even in small ways, such as the creation of a new breed of dog.

Belief #48:
Make No Small Plans, Dream No Small Dreams

How do we come to do what we do? Where do our life goals and dreams originate? On my son, the events of 9/11 have left an indelible mark. Ever since these world-changing events, he has dreamed of becoming a New York City fireman and of rescuing people from burning buildings. Actually, he has modified that dream a bit to include becoming a Chicago firefighter so that he can stay in our beloved city, the Queen of the Midwest.

Others I know are inspired by family—or is it genetics? Two of my design colleagues had grandfathers who were tinkerers and inventors, makers and creators. For me, it was my father who inspired what I do with my life. He spent all of his spare time in his basement shop, making and repairing things for the house and for my school projects, as well as repairing electronics for anyone and everyone to supplement his income. My father was a customs officer, a naval radar technician, a veteran of the Korean War and World War II, and an electronics expert back in the day of vacuum tubes. I wish I had paid attention and learned about electronics from him when I had the chance.

Sadly, I lost him far too young, when I was only fourteen. He stayed up all of his last night with chest pains as his family slept, not wanting to wake us, and in the morning he decided we needed to drive him to the hospital. We never made it; he died in my arms. "DOA," I overheard our pastor tell someone.

My father was a dreamer. He had built a small sailboat before going off to war. I have a photo of it. He was going to sail it around the world, but his mother sold it when he was away at sea and spent the money. My father was an entrepreneur who never had his chance. He saved up his naval earnings ($5,000 was a fortune in the 1940s) to start a business when he returned from the war. His mother spent that, too, while he was fighting for our country.

My father was a motorcyclist. He had an Indian Scout once, and I still recall clearly how he described the sensation of sliding back in the seat as he twisted the throttle and the bike accelerated hard. Because of him, I have known that sensation of sliding back in the seat as my motorcycle accelerates hard, throughout nearly thirty years of riding near and far. Thank you, Dad.

My father was a sailor, and because of him, I wanted to be a naval officer, to serve aboard our ships at sea. And because of him, perhaps, I have always had a craving for being on, near, or living by the water.

My father was a builder with two shops in our basement: one for electronics, where he worked repairing radios to earn money to provide for his family, and a wood shop where he built beautiful things that his family needed. He built our garage, furniture for the house, a giant backyard swing set, and a basketball backboard. Because of my dad, I too am a builder, a maker of things. I cannot imagine life without a shop in which to make and fix. My father knew everything. He could fix anything. He could make anything. I loved him very much, and I miss him still. He helped me dream big and taught me to work hard to make my dreams become reality.

Belief #49:
Jump On Change To Survive

Sesame Street had been in a steady decline in recent years and was being eclipsed by other licenses. It is standard practice in industry to rotate ad agencies, executives, and other personnel to keep things fresh and to prevent getting mired in the entrenched status quo. Mattel and Fisher-Price lost the Sesame Street license when it moved to Hasbro a few years ago. Wow, talk about a sea change in the industry. Change is good. If we keep doing what we have been doing, we will keep getting the exact same results.

It makes sense, in more than one way, for a major licensee to seek a new venue, a new perspective, and a new execution for their flagship brand. Perhaps Hasbro has more to offer, now that they are becoming a force in TV, movies, and entertainment, and can offer a licensee more than a traditional toy company can. One might have wondered why Hasbro was putting so much into recreating itself as an entertainment company. In time, it will become clear whether it was a powerful strategy with profound consequences. What those consequences will be for others in the industry remains to be seen. Change is good. Change is constant. Seek change, or suffer the consequences. The risk of change is smaller than the risk of no change.

We may have been the last organization in the toy industry to get a fax machine. I couldn't see what we would use it for, but was told that once I had one, I would never be able to live without it. (Thank you, Steve.) It was true, and it was one of the first times we adopted a new technology. Our eyes were opened a little to the power of change.

Years later, like a glacier, we began to create better toys with more sophisticated electronics. The change had begun. For years, we had known about servos (motors that can be precisely controlled in speed and degree of movement using a microprocessor), but didn't know how or why we should use them. Instead, we gutted a hundred Billy the Bass units to scavenge their terrific motor mechanisms.

Still later, on the advice of another industry friend, we took the plunge and started to use servos and the basic stamp prototyping electronics system. With the ability to create such precise programming, we were suddenly able to make more sophisticated mechanisms capable of doing remarkable things that would have been impossible before. Our work was transformed by the new tools we had learned to use. Others learned from us to do the same. We became widely known as the "Masters of Mechanisms."

Over the years, other technologies have had significant effects on our capabilities and efficiency, enabling us to create more products of better quality, more quickly and more cheaply. Now we are always looking for the next technology that could transform our business and amplify our capabilities, allowing us to come up with better ideas, build better prototypes, create more sophisticated products, or run our business more efficiently.

Onward and upward, the best is yet to come! Embrace change. Embrace new technologies. Look for ways to transform what you do and how you do it. To survive and thrive in a fast-paced world of business, we have no choice but constant, relentless, and at times, monumental change.

Belief #50:
Just Try It!

Like sharks tracking blood in the water, like a hound dog on a trail, like Sherlock Holmes, we follow our noses, our collective intuition. We are like heat-seeking missiles when we believe we are onto something.

It is a little like baking a cake. We take one of these and combine it with a couple of those: we do things similar to what we have done before, but different. The process starts as an idea. Then a mechanism is crudely cobbled together to see if we like it. Then we bring it to life to see what it can do. Can it do this? Can it do that? Yes? Great! No? Then what if we did this, or tried that? It works? Nah, not so good. Never mind. Let's see if it can… Maybe magnets would help? Add lights? No…try this; see if it works. If it does, good; and if not, that's OK. What else can it do? How can it be even better, and even more amazing? Add the icing on the cake. God is in the details.

"It won't work." I hear that all the time. I think it all the time. Everyone is a critic. Who doesn't love to shoot down someone else's idea? Gosh, that's fun. The problem is, critics don't do things; creators and innovators do things. They change the world around them; critics don't.

"Just try it" is our mantra. In the business of toy invention, we try a lot of things. We create many concepts, but most of them we don't sell. Some of our attempts flat-out just don't work, and that is OK. It is a part of the process of creation, growth, evolution, and learning.

The products we don't license are not failures. Often, years later, we finally do find them a good home with a company for whom they are just right. From each product that we create, we learn something that prepares us to be better and more successful in creating the next product. In trying things that we doubt will work, we accomplish things that seem at times impossible or magical. We didn't think we could get a plush animal to do a cartwheel, but we did: *Tumble Time Tigger*. We didn't think we could get him to do a cartwheel in the package, but we did, and the result was a breakthrough in on-the-shelf package demonstration. We would never have had these successes if we had never tried.

Belief #51:
Just Ride Through It!

Going on a long-distance motorcycle tour can be exhilarating and grueling at the same time. It is a metaphor for life and a metaphor for being in business. I have been going on long-distance bike trips for as long as I have had my business.

Once a motorcycle trip is scheduled, we go rain or shine, hot weather or cold, windy or not. As it is unpredictable, you deal with the weather as it comes. When the day comes, you just ride. Just as in life and in running a business, there are good days, weeks, and months, as well as bad. Ride the waves, ride the bull, hang onto the handlebar grips and just ride through it.

Seven hundred miles in 110-degree heat? Just do it. Rain coming down sideways blown by gale force winds? Put your head down and hang on tight. Persist, in life and in business.

On the road, I never know where I will end up for the night, or even if I'll find a place at all. It's unpredictable, like life and like business. Put your head down, twist the throttle, and put the miles behind you. "Miles to go before I sleep." Hour after hour, hundred miles after hundred miles, through wind and rain, heat and cold, bugs, and traffic. Vibrated, buffeted by the bow-waves of semis and storm gusts, baked under a hot sun, or chilled by a cold wind. Just keep going. See what you see along the way and see where you end up at the end of the day.

On my first solo, long-distance bicycle ride, I rode through a solid week of rain from Amagansett, Rhode Island, to my home in western New York. On my way there, my bike broke down in the mountains of western Massachusetts—the pedal crank bearings broke into pieces. Drenched, with a broken bicycle hoisted up on my shoulder and a wet backpack full of wet clothes, I stood at the base of a large hill and stuck out my hand, hoping against hope that I might get a ride. Miserable and wet, I stood in the rain like a drowned rat with all my belongings on my back, with my thumb out.

Miraculously, someone picked me up. After not too long, a fellow in an International Harvester pickup drove by and told me to throw the bike in the back. He took me to his house, where he and his wife, having grown sons of their own, fed me, dried my clothes, and put me up for the night. A miracle indeed.

But what truly made this a miracle, though, was the town where I happened to end up and what my benefactor happened to do for a living. The town was home to a Schwinn bicycle factory, and the man who picked me up worked there. He took my bike to his bike mechanic friends, and while I slept, they fixed it—enabling me to ride on the next day. Just commit to riding through anything, and you will always weather the storm.

And while I might never be able to repay this debt to those who took me in, I can seek to repay this debt through good deeds and services to others, all the days of my life.

Belief #52:
Do It Because You Can

My motorcycle buddy and I continually discuss why we like to do long motorcycle trips around the country from here to yonder. Out of these talks, here's what I've realized about myself: First, I simply enjoy practicing and perfecting the art of driving a motorcycle. But more importantly, I love setting goals and achieving them. Some goals, such as the pursuit of excellence and constant improvement, have no endpoint. Others can be tied up neatly in a bow; they have a start and an end. Riding my bicycle across the country, motorcycling around all five of the Great Lakes, and training for a power-lifting competition are all goals with a start and a finish.

Next, motorcycling puts me in a state of intense focus: in "the zone." While roaring along, through curve after curve, up and over hill after hill on roads my buddy and I have never ridden, there is the unknown ahead at every bend, whether wildlife, other vehicles, bumps or holes in the road, or pieces of lumber or tire on the road. The hazards are myriad, and we scan ahead with a laser-like intensity hour after hour, curve after curve, hill after hill, so we can immediately respond to any hazard. This is a state of being one does not enter into in ordinary life.

I experience a "oneness" with my machine. Unlike a car and driver, a motorcycle and rider function as a dynamic unit. Cars we steer, accelerate, and brake; bikes we lean with and meld with to become as one.

Riding lets me see things I've never seen and go places I've never been. I have now been intimate with Montana, North Dakota; Idaho was but a brief flirtation as we went through the panhandle only. I've also been through Washington, Oregon, and more. I think I have now been to every state in our great Union, save Alaska and Hawaii.

Then there are the moments of excitement—revving up and passing slower vehicles is always a white-knuckle moment.

Because I can!

Because *you* can! We should all be living life large, grabbing life by the shorthairs, doing what others cannot or will not.

CHAPTER VIII

BELIEF #53:

Walk On The Wild Side

Belief #54:
Live Ridiculous

My life has often been lived on the extemporaneous side. For example, my annual motorcycle trips are not well scripted. I spend the night wherever the day's ride takes me, stop wherever and whenever I want, and take side roads that seem to beckon as I make my way.

On one such ride through the Upper Peninsula of Michigan, before the vast expanses of pristine beaches across the north end of beautiful Lake Michigan, a side road did beckon. It led me and my buddy into the woods and became just a couple of tire tracks that ended at a small, wooded peninsula and an old, long-abandoned lighthouse.

In the top of that lighthouse, we struck up a conversation with a man who had come there to rediscover his family roots. He recounted a most remarkable tale of a zigzag life path and of how his grandfather, from Liechtenstein of all places, had come to America to join his family. As I recall, they were in a community in Iowa or Nebraska.

With just a nickel in his pocket, the grandfather had taken a wrong turn and instead ended up in the Upper Peninsula of Michigan in the middle of winter. Needing to survive but having no money, family, or friends nearby, the man chose to do as many did up there: to cut and sell wood to eke out a living. Lacking money for a horse, he managed to get an old draft harness to wear and became his own horse, dragging the logs out of the woods with his own two feet. He did this until he was able to afford a real horse. As industrious as he was, he was soon able to afford more horses, and over the years, eventually a Caterpillar tractor to increase his yield of lumber.

There was a war on back then, probably World War I, and a little company called Kimberly-Clark needed wood supplies to make paper products. They contracted with the grandfather to keep them supplied, which he did. As they were unable to pay him outright, they paid him in Kimberly-Clark stock. In time, our storyteller's grandfather became the largest holder of Kimberly-Clark stock and eventually became Chairman of the company's Board of Directors. He also became one of the largest landowners in northern Michigan and the UP. He had come a long way from having just a nickel in his pocket and dragging logs out of the woods on foot wearing a worn-out horse harness.

A fortuitous wrong turn it was that took this man to the north woods of Michigan's Upper Peninsula and not to the Liechtensteiner colony in Nebraska. God bless that crooked road that leads us to where we end up, in business, in life, and in love. Know what I mean?

Belief #55:
Take The Road Less Traveled

Take the road less taken sometimes, and you will find it may lead somewhere delightfully unexpected. The road less traveled is the one I often find myself on. (Doesn't that sound like something Yogi Berra might say?)

Life can be well planned or extemporaneous, and of course, it can also be some of both. When I graduated from college, the career path my mother and I both expected me to take (and the one most typical of my peers), was to be law, medicine, or graduate school. I don't think any other options occurred to me at the time. I ended up feeling like I was on a train track—a linear path with few options for my future. So I got off of it. I almost went to Nepal with the Peace Corps, but then I figured that I could always circle back and do that later in life. Who knows…I might do it yet. That was when I chose to become an apprentice leatherworker and learn a craft, a tangible skill, a way to earn a living—whatever the future might hold. My mother disowned me. (But of course, we were poor as paupers, so that was more style than substance.)

Through leatherwork, I rediscovered my love of making things. I found an appreciation of design and problem solving as well as the process of imagination through creation, which was much like what I did throughout high school with science fair projects and model rockets. While my previous study of biology had been the discovery of design in the natural world and the appreciation of nature's most elegant problem solving, I later found that I preferred to create rather than observe.

Lieutenant   "We-are-on-a-first-name-basis-and-my-first-name-is-Lieutenant R" once told me, "Lund, you're digging a hole for yourself," when I left the ROTC program after my most memorable summer at sea. While I don't think that was quite true, I do sometimes wish I had stayed and learned to fly jets off carriers pitching and tossing at sea. I didn't discover my love of going fast until I got my first motorcycle many years later.

Some of us must wander before we can find our paths, and I did find mine. In the words of a country love song by the Rascal Flats, "That God blessed the broken road that led me straight to you." (Flats 2004)

Belief #56:
Live To Work Or Work To Live

At an Australian corroboree (a ceremonial meeting) I was privileged to attend, I had the chance to talk with an esteemed toy industry colleague and competitor, who mentioned that one afternoon when it rained, he had had nothing better to do than sit in bed in his hotel room and watch TV. Perusing the channels, it occurred to him that he couldn't remember the last time he had done that, or had had any downtime at all. Between business, coaching Little League, his wife and kids, and life's other myriad demands, there was no time left for himself. Sound familiar?

I have a couple of other close friends, also industry colleagues, who are A-1 examples of all work and no play. It puts Jack, Ralph, et al in danger of being dull boys. But now, as they pass through their late fifties and sixty looms ahead—a serious age if ever there was one—it has dawned on them that maybe there is more to life than toiling in the vineyard.

We have been given this life to live, the free will to live it as we please, health, and vitality, so why can we not give ourselves permission to live it and love it, fully and exuberantly? Why don't we enjoy it, be lazy, travel, and do for ourselves, not only for others? Live ridiculous, do the unexpected, surprise yourself and others, and make yourself laugh.

Have I been too busy all these years? Am I really going to be so busy, and will the money be so tight, that I cannot see and do the things I've always wanted to do? Is life all about saving for the future, for retirement? What if I don't make it that far? What if the proverbial bus that might hit me tomorrow is out there somewhere? What if it is lying in wait for me so that I won't live long and have to marshal my finances judiciously to make my reserves last at least as long as I do?

Maybe I don't have so long left. Then I saved for what? For nothing? On top of that, I didn't get to see all those wondrous places. I remember a colleague once telling me of his trip to Egypt. He could have said he went to the moon, as likely as it was that I would ever go there. No, not me, for some reason. I may never go to Egypt.

No, can't visit Egypt, or Borneo, or Papua New Guinea—I gotta work. Can't take the time off. "Don't have the money."

Boring. Freakin' boring. BS, in fact.

Another industry colleague always stops in Hawaii for several days of decompression on his way back from trips to Hong Kong and China. He spends the weekend in paradise and arrives back at work in California on Monday, having surfed, relaxed, adjusted time zones, and with a tan. How smart is that? It's genius, I think. (I could never do that. I would have to get home to enjoy my jet lag.)

I spent time with another colleague once who has taken to carrying a sketch book everywhere he goes, to sketch people and places every day. He does it just for himself. It is smart—very smart—to do things like this for ourselves. In caring for our own mental and emotional well-being, we are better able to care for, provide for, love, and cherish those around us.

Belief #57:
Appreciate The Road In The Rearview Mirror

Life is as sweet as honey on the tongue. As we get older and look back, life seems shorter. The years stretch behind us like the road in the rearview mirror as we drive. We have forgotten so much of the journey, we begin to appreciate the limited time we have been given, and that it all will come to an end one day in the not-so-distant future.

My aunt Martha is a wonderful, kind, thoughtful woman with a sparkling wit and rapier-sharp mind. In her late eighties, she has become very frail. On a recent motorcycle trip around Lake Erie, my buddy and I stopped in for a visit. She fixed us lunch and mugged for the camera astride our Harleys. We visited her again a year later when we circumnavigated Lake Ontario. Now she is looking for a home in which to spend the rest of her days. She has an unfailingly humorous take on this most serious next step in her life. If we are lucky to make it to eighty-eight or so, may we each take our next steps with as much grace and equanimity as Aunt Martha.

Belief #58:
Plant The Seeds For The Years To Come

For many years, I attended the toy shows and fairs in the UK, Germany, Hong Kong, and China. Then I quit. I couldn't see sufficient results to justify the time and money spent. I felt that my time in the office, hands-on with product development and in close collaboration with my team, was better spent.

Now I see that the seeds I planted during those travels years ago, the relationships I initiated, are bearing significant fruit. Maintaining those relationships through our Toy Fair meetings, year in and year out, has allowed the seeds to grow and blossom into productive fruit trees from which we now feast, these many years later. Toy Fair is not a time just to see new lines, but to sell, sell, sell new products, develop new relationships, and maintain the precious relationships we already have with others we hope to work with for decades to come.

Everything we do plants seeds for the future. The product is not the thing; the relationship is the thing. And from that, the product will spring.

Belief #59:
Goals Are Like A Ladder: A Tool To Help You Move Higher

A goal is an articulated desire. I have had some memorably successful goal setting experiences, but in general, I have devoted too little time and effort to the laudable practice.

For example, I set a goal to ride my bicycle across the country after college and enlisted a buddy to join me. We trained and we did it. We rode from Carolina to California in thirty-eight days. The next year, I set a goal to ride my bicycle around the world, enlisted a beautiful girl to join me, and didn't go. What was up with that, I wonder? "Sheesh-ka-bibble," my mother might have said. I can't really explain it, but she was oh-so-memorable.

Another time, I set a goal of running a marathon. I hated running before that, and have ever since, but I enlisted a buddy to join me and we trained for a summer. We ran the twenty-six-plus miles in four hours.

See a pattern? Enlisting a buddy to join you is one secret of achieving your goals. Making them specific and measurable is another secret.

Write a blog - and I have been diligently, sometimes more so than others, committing to "paper" my thoughts, observations, and stories on a regular basis for over three years. My goal was to write a book and writing a blog seemed a means to that end by getting me into a habit of writing and it has done just that.

At Lund and Company our goal is excellence in all aspects of our business as well as constant improvement - and while excellence is in itself a goal rather than an achievable end point, I do see year in and year out constant improvement in the work results of our team.

My yearly motorcycle trips were great - but unremarkable for many years. We would ride around Lake Michigan and to southern Illinois - and then we hit upon the idea to do all five of the great lakes and in a matter of a few years we had circumnavigated them all by bike. That has led to setting even larger goals. Our Great Circle Tour of America, riding the perimeter of our great country along north and south borders and along both coasts was kicked off last year.

After that the goal is to ride from Tierra del Fuego to Alaska by motorcycle - about 16000 miles or so - another multi-year ride. And after that perhaps a ride across Australia.

Goals are goo. They can stretch the imagination and take us to places we might not otherwise go. They inspire us to do things both memorable and worth doing that we might not otherwise do. Goals are powerful tools in our lives - like ladders - to allow us to reach higher. Go set some goals for yourself.

CHAPTER IX

BELIEF #60:

A Friend Of A Friend Is My Friend

Belief #61:
Live Large, Dare To Dream

I have known some remarkably creative people who have helped to shape me and my outlook on life. Don't we all carry others around who helped to define who we are? One who comes to mind is my dear, departed friend, Kathleen M. She was a canoeing companion who nearly got us killed in the Rio Grande! She lived in an apartment she affectionately called "The Hovel," behind the garage wherein I had my leather workshop in San Antonio. A feisty, Irish lass with a raw, wicked, irreverent sense of humor that would make me wince, she was a person who knew no fear. You don't meet many who are fearless, but she was. Talk about thinking out of the box. For her, there was no box! She couldn't see any limitations in the world at all. Boxes didn't stand a chance against her.

Kathleen attended college without ever even applying to the school. She just went. She started attending classes and got good grades. Mid-semester, the university discovered that she was not enrolled and had never even applied! They enrolled her immediately so they could at least collect tuition.

Once, Kathleen and her aunt pulled off a scheme to smuggle onyx chess sets and wrought iron furniture from Mexico in a rented cement truck. Now, that was living large, albeit a bit illegally. Whatever did the customs officers think when two youngish women crossed the border from Mexico into the US in a cement truck? I wish I had been there to see it. It was a fascinating plan, worthy of Ralph Kramden of *The Honeymooners*. (Rambling aside, I have always admired smugglers and magicians for their never-ending creative solutions to concealment and misdirection!)

Kathleen would later be proof that the apple doesn't fall far from the tree. Kathleen's aunt, just like Kathleen herself, was bound and determined to get rich. And she did just that. She once dreamt up a scheme to offer the city of San Antonio aerial photography services, for free. Genius...pure genius. Here's how it worked: Everyone loves a good deal, and "free" is hard to pass up. So the City of San Antonio hired Kathleen M's aunt to do aerial photography for them. From the photographs she took, she deduced the direction of the growing city's future development. A very smart woman, she lined up the photos and followed the slow march of urban progression. She figured that if she bought property where the development was planned, it would go up in value! And boy, was she right. Kathleen's aunt became a millionaire from her real estate investments. That is what genius looks like.

This inspired my friend Kathleen. She, too, *had* to become rich. She and her aunt came up with scheme after scheme. Some of them worked famously, and others bordered on the ridiculous. But Kathleen had nerve and nonstop ideas. Later, Kathleen figured the best way to grow filthy rich was to become a lawyer, so off to law school in San Diego she drove one day back in '77.

Since I was going to California to visit a good friend that summer, we shared the trip part of the way. We also planned to stop to canoe the canyons of the Rio Grande River, in Big Bend National Park. Each of these canyons are fifteen or more miles long and fifteen hundred feet deep or more in some places, with sheer walls that rise straight up from the water to the sky.

So Kathleen and I drove hundreds of miles across the deserts of west Texas to put her little aluminum canoe into the Rio Grande River above the canyons. The sky above is a narrow ribbon of blue when you are in the canyons: Boquilla, Santa Elena, and one other. We were going to take several days and do three of the canyons by canoe. We told the park rangers of our plan and struck out for the put-in place at the head of the canyons, many miles across the desert. Little did we know that we were paddling to certain doom!

At a little desert town that felt like a ghost town, we began our three-day adventure. We did not know that a cloudburst upriver had swollen the normally lazy, tranquil waters of the Rio. As we entered the canyons, we were struck by how fast the river was flowing. And as we entered the first canyon, none of it looked familiar.

We had seen many photos of the canyon interior at the ranger station just that morning. Neither did we know that the waters in the canyon can rise fifty feet in an hour as the rain-swollen river is squeezed between the rock walls of the towering cliffs.

Now, rocks the size of a garage that we would have otherwise paddled around were submerged, and the river pouring over such a large rock forms a hydraulic on the other side. Think of it as a wet black hole, into which everything in its path gets sucked. What looked like an improbable shadow in the river ahead was actually a gaping maw, a steep-walled hole wider than the length of our canoe. I actually thought we might jump across it since we were moving so fast.

I remember it vividly, almost in slow motion. The canoe tipped sideways as it dove into the blackness, the belly of the beast. Then it was like being in a washing machine full of brown water—around and around, not knowing up or down, and thus not knowing what to do or where to swim, banging on the bottom of the river. No idea of how to save yourself, you begin to accept that this might be the end. But a hydraulic, sooner or later, pops everything back up, and pushes out everything that goes down into it. This one popped us back out as well. I clawed my way out of the water and onto a protruding rock, dizzy and exhausted.

After barely surviving being sucked into a hydraulic, I would have been content to sit on that rock for the next three days if need be, until help might finally come, but not Kathleen! She wanted to jump into that raging river and swim the fifteen or so miles out of the canyon (after we had just barely escaped drowning). It was a crazy idea, but we tried it. We immediately got into trouble and had to find a sandbar to drag ourselves out again. The current was way too swift. Help did finally arrive as night set, and we were saved.

Yes, we survived that adventure, but only barely. The park rangers, hearing of the downpour upriver, had set out to intercept us if possible. They had floated down the river by raft, looking for our bodies, they said. Like a pair of near-drowned rats, we were rescued just as darkness fell, and lived to tell the tale.

I lost touch with Kathleen for many years, but spoke to her one more time. Kathleen moved to the Pacific Northwest, started a fishery, became an assistant attorney general, and a slum landlord (her words), and had already survived breast cancer and diabetes. When she finally succumbed to cancer, she was in the process of starting an airline. She was relentless, she was without fear; she was full of ideas, energy, laughter, and sarcasm. She was one remarkable human being, and I will always miss her. She dreamed big. She lived large. I do miss you, Kathleen, and hope to see you again one day. And I intend to live large from now on, inspired by you.

Belief #62:
A Smile And A Sparkling Wit Ensure A Long Life

It was a great honor and a pleasure to have the toy and game inventor legend Reuben Klamer, along with his family and friends, come to our offices for a visit. We went to the legendary Margie's Candies for some grilled cheese sandwiches, hot fudge sundaes, and chocolate milkshakes. That is my idea of a great meal. It turns out that Reuben, with his youthful spirit, impish smile, and a sense of humor as fresh as tomorrow, is crazy about chocolate milkshakes, and hot fudge sundaes, too. You gotta love a man like that.

Our friendship goes back a long time, and we have long been great admirers of each other's work. Reuben created the Milton Bradley classic The Game of Life, which in 2010 celebrated its fiftieth anniversary. He has also licensed over two hundred other products, over a career that spans decades.

Reuben was in Chicago receiving a lifetime achievement award from the Chicago Toy and Game Fair that was richly deserved and well earned. He also autographed a couple of versions of his Game of Life for us and I autographed and gave him one of our *TMX Elmos*. I should blush at the superlatives he used in the notes he penned on the game boxes.

Rueben has a sparkling wit, and beatific warmth that emanates from him like a toy industry saint. Turns out he is writing a book about his life.

During dinner, Reuben told us the story of how the Hula Hoop came to be. A friend sent him an Australian aboriginal stick and reed hoop that he thought could be translated into a new plastic: long-chain polyethylene, a material that Reuben had introduced to the toy industry and made him famous, opening many doors in his early years. Prior to Reuben, plastic toys had been made of styrene, a hard and brittle plastic prone to cracking and breaking into sharp shards. Polyethylene was soft and unbreakable. His toy industry breakthrough was inspired by an ad for a soap bottle that could be dropped and would bounce without breaking.

It turns out that a few other people who saw Reuben's stick and reed hoop knew about his new plastic, as well. As I heard him tell it, these other individuals popularized the concept as the Hula Hoop, and the rest is history. It began in Reuben's shop, however, with an aboriginal hoop sent by a friend, and ended up being made of the plastic he "discovered" for the toy industry. The original Australian hoop still hangs in his office.

When I asked him further about one of the stories he told us that evening, he responded, "Buy the book!" When I asked him when he would finish the book, he said, "No idea! I don't give a s***!" chuckling like Santa's head elf with a perfectly elfish twinkle in his eye. No wonder I love that man.

His first toy licensed? Moon Rocks, now known as Magic Rocks. In addition to the Game of Life from over fifty years ago, he also invented hundreds of other well-known and unknown products, among them the Fisher-Price Grow With me 1, 2, 3 Roller Skates, on which millions of kids first learned to skate.

Reuben is bright eyed, and has an angelic demeanor. He is warm, kind, extraordinarily funny and clever, sharp as a tack, and actually closer to eighty-six in age at this writing. He is still inventing and licensing toys and games. I hear he even has a business partner he works with who is in his nineties. Reuben, retire already. Give the rest of us a chance! But he won't. He still loves doing it.

Belief #63:
Life Is But A Moment; Make It Count

Not long ago, my family was reeling from the loss of the son of our dear friends. He was adopted from Paraguay at the same time as my son and was only seventeen when he died. We have photos of him and my son as infants lying side by side on a blanket in the yard of the Asuncion hotel where adoptive parents stayed until they were able to bring their babies home, a process that usually took about two weeks. In some cases, it took up to nine months, and in others, tragically, the babies were never allowed to leave with the adoptive parents. But that is a tale for another day, perhaps.

His parents are wonderful, decent, God-fearing, and devout people. They are selfless and generous. Over the years, they have been like angels in the lives of my family and of many others' as well. Their son was vivacious, enthusiastic, loving, and well loved. He was junior class president, a singer and performer, a devout child of God, a fine and beautiful young man, and was gone in his sleep before he could even enter the prime of his life.

I cannot imagine how his parents go on, one foot in front of the other, after the loss of their precious eldest son. I do not know how any parent manages after the loss of a child.

The world manages to go on without him, as it will go on one day without each of us, I suppose. But the world and the many lives he was a part of seem somewhat emptier for this young man's absence. It feels as if a weight has settled upon our hearts. In time, it will lift, no doubt. I tell my son that life is about loss; that we will lose much and many that we love. From loss, perhaps, even briefly, we appreciate what we have. Our sons and daughters, friends and family, our dogs, and our own existence: all are momentary, though we live as if they were cast in steel.

Belief #64:
Surround Yourself With Shining Examples Of Love

My dog Roxy, may she rest in peace, was a bright light that came into our lives at a time of sadness for my family. She was eternally happy, she loved unconditionally, and she greeted each of us on our return at the end of a day with whimpers and a furiously wagging body and tail, as if we had been gone for weeks, or months, or years. She would wag her tail off, and we would have to put it back on again with duct tape and safety pins at least once a week.

Actually, she would beat the walls so hard with her tail that it would sometimes bleed, and we'd have bloody streaks on walls throughout the house. Our side entry door was where she most often greeted us all with boundless, tail-damaging enthusiasm. That is what dogs are all about. Our options were to amputate that great big, black club of a tail; wrap it in foam pipe insulation to protect it (which did not work, by the way); or learning the art of tail management (in other words, not letting her beat her tail against anything!). The latter worked just fine.

While Roxy may have been stupid about taking care of her tail, she was a very smart dog overall. Such a smart girl. Such a happy girl. "My Baby Girl" is what my son would call her. We adored her. Everyone fell in love with Roxy. If she had been a woman, I would have married her in an instant. Every friend or visitor to the home would remark on her, and some frequent visitors were also greeted with her over-abundant happiness and tail-thumping love. What a beautiful crea-ture was our Roxy Anne. Good Lord, what a dog! I am astonished at how much we miss her. We keep expecting to hear her footsteps and her bark, to see her come padding around the corner, as if she is only away and will return. I guess we are in denial.

One day when she was getting old, I noticed that she was breath-ing differently, breathing harder. But I was in the midst of several weeks of travel, and took too little notice of it, perhaps. When I returned home briefly before leaving again, I learned that Roxy was not eating her dry food with her accustomed gusto. Being a Labrador retriever, she was very…"food motivated," I think is the term. She would eat anything, anytime, and always acted as if she were on the brink of starvation. I don't want to even go into the things she would eat if you weren't watching. Yuck! Yecch!

While I was away again, she lay down on the ground during a walk and would not get up again. So Roxy went in to the vet. I got the call that night while still in transit. I had expected her to get medicine and be good as new by the next day when I returned, but that was not to be. The vet later said she needed to be monitored overnight and to be transported to a hospital, as she was in criti-cal condition. Critical condition? That cannot be! What were they talking about?

In the morning, when I half expected to go bring her home, they told me to come in and spend some time with her. She was not getting better, but worse. She was too sick for the animal internist to even examine to determine what was wrong, and the X-rays were not clear, other than showing one lung filled with fluid.

When I arrived at the animal hospital to see Roxy for the last time, she wagged that beautiful tail, smiled her heart-stopping smile, and got up to greet me as she always did. We sat together for a while. I got her boy—now really a young man—on the phone to tell her how much he loved her. They put Roxy and me in a private room where I could sit with her, talk to her, and pet her, letting her know it was OK to go, though we would miss her so. After less than an hour, she laid her head back on my foot as she breathed her last and her great big, loving, overflowing-with-happiness heart stopped.

I cried, and cry again writing this. She is gone forever. If ever a dog should go to heaven, all the heavenly hosts would welcome one such as she.

I am inspired by our Baby Girl. I wish I could be half as happy, even half of the time, as Roxy was all the time. She never asked for a thing. Oh, maybe she would plead to stay out a little longer when I was bringing her in—and there was no resisting those pleading eyes—but she was always happy.

She was and is a shining example of love, of how to love intensely and uncritically. That is perhaps the route to happiness. Roxy was never angry, never held a grudge, never showed envy or any of the seven deadly sins. Well, at least not five…or maybe four of them. She was a glutton, surely. But so what? And she was sloth-ful, maybe, as she lived a life of ease. But the others, no. Lust was not a problem, as she had been spayed even before we adopted her.

I will never forget the day we went "only to look" and came home with this great big beast of a black lab who stole our hearts in time. Roxy was a saint of a creature, and an example of a loving, happy heart. I wish I could be more like her, and I will try to be. God bless you, Roxy, wherever you are, and thank you, Lord, for bringing her into our lives. Amen.

Belief #65:
Be Open To New Friends Of Any Variety

They really should do a TV reality show about Hillsborough, North Carolina. It's quiet and quaint, but a seething cauldron of violence and malevolence used to lie beneath the surface. There have been a lot of stories in that little town, and many are still going on, I would bet. My friends, the "C" family, lived on the other side of town. They owned a lumberyard in town and lived in a 1700s vintage home full of priceless cloisonné vases from the Ming dynasty (and probably every other dynasty, as well).

Theirs was a most unusual variation on quiet country living. Mrs. C was a psychic, a neighbor and friend of Dr. J. B. Rhine and his wife, who was also a psychic and able to call her children to dinner telepathically from miles away. Dr. Rhine founded the Rhine Research Center for Parapsychology at Duke, the first of its kind.

And the C's lives were full of odd animals and myriad ghostly apparitions of an endless variety, though sadly, never when I was visiting. They had a ghost cat that one might see out of the corner of the eye, flitting from room to room. At a party once, a cat fight broke out in the middle of the room, but only one cat could be clearly seen. The other appeared as a gray, cloudy, indistinct shape. Furniture would inexplicably move; dishes would fly to the center of the room and drop to the floor. Cats would suddenly gather, mewing with distress and rubbing against your leg, often just before something odd happened.

When the family was working on the house before moving in, they noted that it had a "cold heart." Often reported in haunted houses, this was a cylinder of air noticeably colder than the rest of the room. And they had a dark closet that none of the workers would go into. Shining a flashlight into its gloom had little effect, and if you put the flashlight in the closet and shone it back at yourself, you could see only a dim light.

One day a prolonged creak, followed by a loud crack, as if of a large timber, was heard by all. And the cold heart was gone, the dark closet no longer dark. But this was by no means the end of odd events and occurrences. Mrs. C was unafraid, as she felt the spirits were friendly. In the "borning room," where generations of babies had in fact been born, the family reported that one might often hear murmuring, the faint sound of teacups and saucers perhaps, and the cooing of women who might have gathered to admire a new baby just born into the world.

My schoolmate Bob, their youngest son, thought his older brother was pounding on the bathroom door one day, spouting obscenities at him for taking so long, only to find that his brother was not at home. I always hoped and feared I might experience just one tiny, ghostly event, but it did not happen. I still do, actually. The next house I buy is going to be haunted.

Other than the spirits picking up Mrs. C and spinning her around one day, which she didn't like at all (and it was the first time she was scared), my favorite was the misty appearance of handprints on one of the family's antique cabinets. Each day, two sets of prints would appear, one over the other. The bottom set appeared to be those of a small child; those above were adult, but with spider fingers, each having an extra joint. The anomaly was perhaps another artifact of inbreeding. The area was reported to contain the largest degenerate gene pool in the south, with inbreeding for many generations. One day, as Mrs. C was about to wipe off the prints, they began to move. They slid down and off the face of the cabinet, vanishing, never to appear again.

I always wanted a brick or a board from that house, so that if a ghost remained in association with it, I could store it in a safe deposit box and rent it to people who wanted a ghost in their own home. "Rent a Ghost," I would call my new business! I think it could be a franchise if I could just get enough pieces of haunted houses.

Just outside this quaint, sleepy-seeming town of Hillsborough was the rural community of Frog Level, the T-intersection where I apprenticed at the leatherwork shop in a converted country store building at the center of the rag-tag community. Quiet though Hillsborough seemed, violence was never far away.

My mechanic, Fred, was originally from Maine. He spoke with a Maine accent on top of his adopted home state's southern accent. Combined with his almost constant drunkenness, one really couldn't understand a word he said. It was as if he talked in some unknown language. But folks said he was an auto-mechanic savant, a genius. Could work miracles on any vehicle. Well, my 1951 Willy's Jeep pickup truck dream vehicle had never run once after I bought it. It sorely needed some miracles. To pay Fred (and I know you will wonder what I was thinking), I would take him to the ABC store each morning for a bottle of cheap liquor and instruct him not to drink it until after he did the work. Each afternoon I'd come by, and Fred was nowhere to be found. Duh!

Needless to say, no work was ever done, and my dream wheels never rolled again. Go ahead and look up *dumb* in the dictionary if you want to see my photo!

Years later, I learned that Fred met a tragically ironic end when the car he was driving down Orange Grove Road (while drunk, of course), collided head-on with another car. It killed that driver as well, who was also drunk. The driver of that other car was Fred's wife. They did each other in: a tragic comedy, a poetic end.

Some of the violence out at Frog Level, but by no means all, originated with a couple of ex-cons who had done time in the "slammer" together. They hated and vowed to kill one each other and threatened each other's families. Sometimes they did more than threaten, in ways that are not suitable for sharing in this volume.

I lived a ways down a dirt road in what some might call a shack. It had no running water, or even an outhouse, but it cost only $15 a month. My good friend Bill B, who now lived next door, had raised his family in this shack. His son lived across the street. The only insulation on the shack's wood siding was some newspaper nailed between interior two-by-fours.

My water I kept in a plastic garbage can. Since my wood stove was shot full of holes and wouldn't stay hot through the night, I would have to break a thin layer of ice on winter mornings and dip in a pan for water to make coffee or hot chocolate to warm up. You should have seen David and me fill my garbage can from his well and carry it back up the deeply rutted hill in the back of his pickup truck, sloshing wildly. I almost always got at least a half-filled garbage can of water. And without my electric blanket, I'd have died. My "backyard" looked like a junkyard in the woods, full of rusting old cars, trucks, and major appliances that Bill would use as storage lockers for his moonshine or homemade wine (that sometimes looked more like milk).

I wanted to be a hermit, write, and study karate seriously. I didn't do either of the last two, and decided being a hermit just wasn't for me. So after a year or so, I moved back into town.

Belief #66:

Everyone Has A Story To Tell, If We Will But Listen

My friend Bill was also the strongest man I ever knew, with arms the size of my thighs. I first met him when I was a freshman at Duke. He worked in the university's greenhouses, every day of the week, every week of the year, every year. For him, there were no vacations, holidays, weekends, or days off. He had always worked hard. And when he was younger, it was for only fifty cents a week. It's hard to believe that he worked sunup to sundown on a neighboring farm for that, even as a boy. Years later, his son David recalls working his first real job for ninety cents an hour. It's hard to get ahead or even feed a family on those wages. At the dinner table, he would take no food. After everyone else had eaten, he would scrape the leftovers onto his plate, and that would be his meal. Only decades later did his family realize that Bill had done this because they had had so little food and no money to buy more. Their Daddy lived on what was left over. This was a father's love.

Bill had always been strong, maybe even unnaturally so. Down on the farm, they would use young Bill like a piece of equipment. If a tractor got stuck in the mud, they'd call him to come pull it out. In the Marines, Bill was quiet and kept to himself. One night, a rowdy game of cards was going on in the barracks and keeping Bill awake. Annoyed, he finally called out "Y'all boys makin' too much noise." His fellow Marines had so much respect for the strength of my friend Bill that they went quiet enough to hear the proverbial pin drop. He was not one you'd want to cross, mild mannered though he was.

On another occasion, a judo instructor was out on the parade grounds showing off, challenging men to try to defeat him. A crowd of Marines had gathered, and as Bill walked by, they called him over. He resisted, they insisted; in a trice he was in the ring with this little judo instructor, who had been tossing men much larger than he on their keisters!

And in another moment, the judo instructor was picked up overhead and thrown up and over the heads of the ring of observers, landing with a thud. He bounced and rolled. Picking himself up, he ran off, soundly and roundly defeated. Bill was amazingly strong.

I remember another story about a sergeant who used to lift weights out on the parade grounds, showing off all the weight he could press overhead and dead-lift. Out of curiosity, one day Bill went out to see how heavy the weights were. The first barbell was the one the sergeant used for an overhead, two-handed military press. Bill—picture this—picked it up, and with arm straight out, brought it up overhead and pressed it several times with just one arm. The other barbell was much heavier and was used for dead lifts: lifting to a standing position only and back down. Bill picked up this much heavier weight and did an overhead press with it a few times before putting it down, unimpressed.

The sergeant was never seen to touch those weights again. Perhaps he was mortified that Bill had made them look like they weighed nothing at all! Bill was indeed a mighty strong man. But Bill had a friend who was even stronger. This rural southern farmer worked out in an abandoned chicken coop with a set of weights he had welded together. While working on the railroad, he once bet his coworkers that he could pick up a twelve-hundred-pound length of rail that normally took ten men or more to carry. With homemade leather straps around it, he dead lifted the rail, squatting over it and standing up straight. I struggle to dead lift three hundred pounds, myself.

Years later, I came back to that dirt road where they both had lived and inquired of some of the remaining neighbors after Bill and his friend, and asked about their stories. Yep, it was all true. "That was when men was men," one neighbor said, and I quote.

And Bill's friend, the dirt farmer from Hillsborough, North Carolina, was even featured on the *Tonight Show* with Johnny Carson twice, so strong was he! He complemented Bill once, telling him "Bill, you could be strong too, if you would work out."

Belief #67:

Live Life Fully, And Suck Out The Marrow From The Bones

Abe was a good friend for the years that we worked together. We never made any money, but I surely enjoyed his company. He was a man's man. He loved to do things that today are seen askance and discouraged—but if not for some vices, we are in danger of becoming boring, don'tcha think? In fact, Mark Twain tells the story of a man on his deathbed. The doctor tells him that if he is to survive, he has to give up smoking, drinking, and chasing women.

The man replied "I already have," and promptly died. You've got to have some vice to give up when your time comes!

Abe, too, pursued all the fine hobbies just described. He was a scuba diver with a style he described metaphorically as "sitting in the garden and watching the flowers swim by." He had been a heavy equipment mover, a soldier in the Israeli army, had lived on a commune, and so on.

When the town zoning restrictions where he lived limited where he could build his garage, he built the whole thing *on wheels* so that he could move it! Crazy. Each Saturday, he opened his garage and invited neighbors near and far to bring him cars, computers, toys—anything and everything that needed to be repaired. All for free.

What a man, my friend Abe.

Belief #68:
You Never Know Who You'll Meet On Life's Highway

On a cross-country bike journey once with a buddy, I rode into the little town of War, West Virginia. And the town was buzzing. There were kids everywhere, many with rifles on their shoulders, as they rode their banana seat bikes with one hand. The sidewalks were crowded with men, women, and children, all seemingly armed. For a couple of long-haired college grads on a long-distance bike ride, this did not seem like a welcome committee!

One group of men, all holding firearms of wide variety, hailed to us loudly as we attempted to speed up without a pause, just to get through this little hornet's nest of armed activity. We tried to ignore the hailers, but they persisted. So we pulled over to see what they wanted with us.

The one who'd hailed us down was Rocky O (I remember his name to this day). He told us the tale of what had riled up his otherwise sleepy little town. Some days earlier, there had been a prison break down in Georgia, and the escapees had managed to rape, plunder, and pillage their way north until they were stopped at a roadblock by the state police on the road leading west out of War. The escaped convicts abandoned their car and had run up into the steep, wooded hills of West Virginia. Hearing of this, the citizenry of War took up arms and headed up into the hills after them.

Meanwhile, the state police had found the escapees asleep in a small cave, where they quietly surrendered. The police remarked that those boys were lucky the law had found them first.

In the aftermath of the drama, the town was still abuzz with high energy and armed to the teeth. Assuring us that we were not in danger and explaining the presence of so many guns to our satisfaction, Rocky invited us home to dinner and offered a place to sleep for the night. A miner like his father (and likely his sons as well), he was short and wide, with an enormous bushy, black beard. He looked like a dwarf king from one of the *Lord of the Rings* movies.

Rocky's family were building a seven-story "skyscraper" home next to their current home, but after seven years into the project they had only a steel I-beam skeleton two and a half stories high. I didn't see that they would ever complete it.

Rocky shared his West Virginia hospitality (he taught us how to rapidly descend a steep slope if we should need to outrun a bear!) and sent us on our way the next day. We got on our bikes and headed west. Ironically, the next town we encountered was called Justice. It had been served just twenty-four hours earlier and fifteen miles down the road!

There have been other characters in my life of course, and I'm sure there will be more to come. These are a few who stand out in my mind. They helped to shape my beliefs and the person I am today. I hope to fill the pages of Volume II with many other such tales. I'm sure you have a few to tell of those you carry around—in your mind, on your back, in your heart—those who define who you are.

CLOSING

"So what?" you ask. What now? What does this all mean for you and for me? What should you do differently, now that I have finished writing this book, and now that you have read it?

I don't have a prescription for you of course. Heck, I am still working on my own. This is a lifelong process, and if you are like me, you may not begin in earnest until the second half of your life. The first half I probably spent cruising along in a state of complacency, not realizing my potential for improvement in all aspects of my life.

But there are some things that I have learned, as I mentioned. There are some simple concepts that I can recommend and that I have found to yield results over time.

Believe in yourself. Identify what you believe in. Discover your core beliefs. Find out what you love, what you do that gives your life meaning, gives you joy—and do as much of it as you can. A life lived without joy and pursuit of happiness is not a life worth living. To do anything great, first you must love doing it.

What I love is leatherwork, inventing toys and games, weight-lifting, and working closely with a team of people that I respect and enjoy. I love motorcycling hither, thither and yon; and more recently again, scuba diving and coming face to face with the spectacular variety of creatures that lives beneath the oceans' waves.

The products that we have created over the years are the result of acting according to our beliefs. We are still in business because I am not very good at giving up, or quitting, or throwing in the towel. As I've said, I believe that persistence overcomes all things. We licensed *Honey My Baby Pony*, twelve years (or more) after it was originally created, because we persisted. That product eventually led to the very successful Animagic line, with my dear friends and colleagues at Vivid Imaginations in the UK. *Doggie Doo* and our *Pictionary Bend-a-Clues* game both took fifteen years and scores of rejections before we were able to license them. I think that might be fairly called persistence!

We have had bad years when we hemorrhaged money, threatening me and mine with financial ruin. We announced the closure of the business forever on a Friday, cutting staff and expenses by 50 percent. We reopened again on Monday with a renewed sense of purpose and joy in the challenge of survival. We not only survived, but in time we thrived, creating some of the best products in our history.

We skated close to the edge again recently—precariously close, due to a perfect storm of nearly catastrophic events, both macro- and microeconomic in scale. But even as I write, some of our new products this year are already being reported sold out in Big Box and ma-and-pa stores alike. We are on track to have one of our best years ever. Next year looks even brighter still.

On more than one occasion, cowardly curs, knaves, and foreign scoundrels have absconded with our concepts. We have suffered through the numerous bankruptcies of our client toy companies, losing millions in monies already due and payable, and in the lost sales of products that fell by the wayside as a result. We spent years throwing good money after bad, hiring attorneys and waging legal battles to collect our ten cents on the dollar of whatever was left of these bankrupt toy companies, wherever possible. Yet again, we lived to tell the tale.

Over the years, many of our associates have been poached by our competitors, and curiously, concepts that we had in-house then appeared on the market under license from the very companies our former associates had joined. Again, and again. Coincidence? Maybe? Maybe NOT! One competitor in particular is populated with those we plucked from obscure jobs and trained in the art of being toy inventors. Ah, well. So it goes.

Still, we live to tell the tale and to fight again another day. Is this persistence? Or stupidity? Perhaps failure of the imagination to come up with another way to make a living? Nah. I just love what I do, and want to be freakin' great at it! It's the simple desire to let the others eat my dust. And for a precious few, perhaps, the chance one day to dance on their graves.

We believe in constant change, and constant improvement. We have committed ourselves to greatness, and to achieve it is a process rather than a destination. Because we seek constant improvement, each year we do indeed get better at what we do. And what we create today is far better than what we created ten or even seven years ago– recognizably better.

Who wouldn't want to get better and better? We must change and get better at what we do in business to survive, or we die. Simple as that.

We don't believe in "impossible." Even when we think something can't be done, we try to put the belief to the side and approach a solution to a worthy problem as if we believed it *were* possible. *Tumble Time Tigger* doing a cartwheel in the box, *TMX Elmo* doing it all with only two motors, and to top that, the *TMX Friends* that followed who were capable of doing all that and more—with only one (I repeat, ONE) motor, are all examples of mechanical engineering triumphs that we had once believed impossible. And with good reason. Anyone skilled in the "arts," to use patent office lingo, would think that what we attempted—and succeeded in— was impossible.

We are persistent *in* constant improvement. Year after year, we continue to explore simple technologies in depth. This leads us to observations and discoveries, going "where no one has gone before," doing things rational thought labels as impossible, yet "whoomp," there it is.

Our team has a magical spirit of cooperation, mutual support, and appreciation. It is a synergy of skills and abilities, generously shared. It is something to see in action, because, as I have noted, you can't point to it. This team spirit allows our several ordinary intellects to combine and function as one gigantic freakin' genius-level intellect. Together, a team can do what no individual can.

Good teamwork is the secret to all championships in the world of sports, and not surprisingly, in the world of business as well. Not individual stars, but the intentional intermeshing of capable, competent, and dedicated individuals, striving toward common goals, can yield spectacular results. Without the mechanical capabilities of one member, the electronics knowledge of another, and the programming expertise of a third, a *TMX Elmo* or so many of our other products would not have been possible.

Teamwork is external as well as internal. The whole rest of the world can be on your team. *Uno Roboto* was the result of close collaboration with a client company's internal team, along with our esteemed colleagues at Random Games, another highly regarded game design group. The line of TMX characters and *Tumble Time Tigger* achieved their level of greatness from a similar close collaboration. Next year's likely Toy of the Year will also be the result of a great collaboration between our team and our client partner.

Importantly, team members don't just help. They can be most valuable in challenging us to make our products even better and more amazing. In many cases, they have pushed us to do the impossible (being naturally lazy, we would rather not tackle the impossible, of course). And doing the seemingly impossible is what pushes a very good product to the level of great.

In the years ahead, you will see some amazing gizmos, contrivances, contraptions, mechanisms, and way-cool actions. These will be based on an age-old technology being explored in depth, hand in hand with yet another of our partner toy company's internal teams. Prepare to be amazed at the innovation in yet another product category. But none of this could come into existence without the teamwork of which I speak. Teamwork is the key to realizing the impossible. And I would like to add that we work hard because we know this. We have seen that the greater the effort is, the greater the results. Makes sense that it should work that way, eh?

We collaborate…to create…the great. (My mother was a poet. All my rhymes are my tribute to her.) We try things. We try them knowing that many won't work—or that they may work, but will never find a home. That is OK. Without taking a chance, without trying things that may or may not work, may or not be successful, or may or not get licensed and see the light of day on a retailer's shelf, we will never create what will one day be a success.

Our *Hydrogen-Powered Rocket System* started as a whim: try electrolysis, and see what it suggests. The first consumer product powered by hydrogen was born, and sold for almost a decade. The first new toy rocket technology to hit the market in nearly fifty years led to a multiyear project for the Department of Defense on what has been described as a revolutionary new system for varying the velocity of nonlethal projectiles.

Success is built on a foundation of failures, or perhaps more accurately, unsuccessful efforts. Just try it.

Even now, we are trying to evolve our business, to change and to grow by an order of magnitude. Our efforts have already borne fruit. Recent goals have included new product lines and new brands, not just items that fill a hole in someone else's line. The Animal Plush, Tigger and Elmo products are good and sales may be impressive, but only for six months or so, as they are destined to be replaced every year by a new pretty face—the new "key driver" that drives sales of the rest of the brand not supported by TV promotion. Like the soldier that leads the charge up the hill, these key drivers always take the bullet, to be replaced with a new one the following year.

Our *Little Miss Muffin* line, much of the Animagic range, and our *Flufflings* line are evidence that we can create and sell lines of product rather than just individual items, potentially creating new brands that can sell year after year and generate as much or more than a single blockbuster item.

So, what does this all mean? Yes, toys do matter. They are important! I've maintained that through play with toys and games in particular, children learn how to behave and interact effectively with others. Though the evidence is anecdotal, it is quite clear that toys can and do change the world. Toys influence what we do with our lives, the work that we choose, and ultimately, the contributions we make to the world and the lives of others. As noted, the Wright Brothers and Frank Lloyd Wright have said just that. Perhaps you, too, have been influenced to do what you do in your adult life by the toys of your childhood. Perhaps the world will be a different place as a result.

Toys matter. To buy a toy is an investment in joy! Buy a toy and change the world. Go out and buy a toy today!

ACKNOWLEDGMENTS

Writing this book has been a very satisfying project. I have long wanted to write a book, but had no idea what to write about. I didn't think I would have the discipline to sit for the hours needed to write a book from start to finish, so busy is my life.

So this book, the realization of a dream, has been a team effort from the start. It began with a blog I didn't know why I was writing. But so much of what we do in toy invention is to try things and see if they work. If they don't, then we try something else. But because I wanted to write a book, I reasoned that writing anything was a step in the "write" direction. And my reasoning proved sound. In time, I would know if the efforts of writing a blog would bear fruit.

And they have. The blog posts I wrote became the material for this book. They were musings on life and business, recollections, and lessons from my thirty-two-plus years in the toy business. Our esteemed Cassie and just amazing Jessie collected and stitched them together into their current form. It has been very much a collaborative team effort.

So, first, thanks to Cassie, as I would not have begun the blog long ago, nor this tome you now hold in your hands, without her encouragement, support, and continued efforts toward its completion and publishing. Cassie, you are wonderful!

Second, I want to thank Jessie for her posting of the blog each day and enhancing my words with images and links that bring them to life and add interest and appeal for potential readers. Ridiculously reliable, and always working with grace and equanimity no matter the stress and strain of the day, Jessie, you are a Godsend.

I want to thank my father for giving me the gift of experiencing joy through making things. It was in his basement shop where I was most at home and learned to love the use of tools, the fabrication processes and materials, the noise, and the mess on the floor. I also learned the process from imagination through creation to realization: the process of bringing something new into the world, where there had earlier been only potential.

I want to thank my mother for the pithy pearls of wisdom that I call upon often to guide my thinking and behavior. "Oh, for the gift that God could give us, to see ourselves as others see us" has always been one of my favorites. It helps me to judge more gently the behavior of others, as they surely judge me less gently than I might wish. And "Oh, but by the Grace of God go I" comes to mind whenever I see the homeless, the disabled, and the infirm; I know that I do not earn my blessings any more than others deserve their misfortunes. It causes me to pray quietly to myself that the Good Lord hold this person, or those unfortunates, gently in the palm of his hand, and to thank him for my multitude of blessings. I miss my parents both.

I have been blessed to know many fascinating people and have longed to share their stories with others, some of which have become part of the fabric of this book. Others will have to wait for another volume. I would like to thank Stu, the most creative person I ever met, who set me up in my first business down in Chapel Hill, North Carolina. He taught me leatherwork, he taught me about aesthetics, and he taught me to appreciate fine craftsmanship and so much more. He taught me how to "make s*** and sell it," which I have been doing ever since. Thank you, old friend.

I thank the many coworkers and Lund and Company colleagues who have toiled beside me over the years like so many magnificent horses harnessed with me in the same traces, pulling the same great wagon. Among them are Mike, Jessie, Krishnan, Cesar, Guruge, Lowell, Bugman, Jo753, Bret, Trish, and many others. I thank the wonderful friends, too numerous to all mention here, that I have known and loved along the way: brave, strong, wise, loving, hilarious, creative, and beautiful creatures all.

And finally, I thank my beautiful Tara and my two wonderful children, Jonathan and Jacquelin, who represent to me the very meaning of life and joy, and the basis for this book.

And you, the reader, if you have gotten this far on the page, I thank you for your time and interest. I do truly wish that some benefit be conferred on you as a result of your time spent with the words I have written and the tales I have told.

And while last on this page, in truth it is first and foremost: I thank the Good Lord above for the hands with which I write, the eyes with which I see, the body which carries me about from here to there, the chance to walk this earth for a time and partake of its joys and sorrows, and to have the chance to strive to make a difference, to leave this world in some small way better for my having been here. I devote my work to the glory of God and the benefit of his peoples.

Bruce D. Lund

WORKS CITED

Benson, Etienne. "Leggo of the Lego!, The Erector set rises again." *Popular Science,* December 2010.

Brosterman, Norman. *Inventing Kindergarten.* 1st edition. Harry N. Abrams Books, 1997.

Brown, Stuart. "Taking Play Seriously." *New York Times Magazine,* September 2, 2009.

Gray, Peter. "The Decline of Play and the Rise of Psychopathology in Children and Adolescents." *American Journal of Play* Volume 3, no. Number 4 (Spring 2011).

Juster, F. Thomas et al. "Study: Changing Times of American Youth - 1981-2003." *Institute for Social Research, University of Michigan, Child Development Supplement,* 2004.

Papanek, Victor. *Design for the Real World.* 2 revised edition. Chicago: Academy Chicago Publishers, 2005.

Rascall Flats. "Bless The Broken Road." *Feels Like Today.* ASIN B0002VL0Z6. 2004. Audo CD.

Wang, Shirley. "The Power of Magical Thinking, Research Shows the Importance of Imagination in Children's Cognitive Development." *Wall Street Journal,* December 22, 2009.

Made in the USA
Charleston, SC
07 July 2012